The Equine Semaphore Code

the horse talks back

Meljay Turner

This book belongs to:

____

Meljay Turner

Meljay Turner is a loving and devoted mother of three, a thrill-seeker who has gripped the rails of the roller-coaster of life and is still screaming her joy as she speeds through the barrel rolls and loop-the-loops. Meljay has travelled the greatest adventure of life, motherhood, and now that her children are grown she is on a new adventure that few have travelled before her.

Author of this first time, first of its kind publication, Meljay delves deeper into the equine language than anyone has dared before. The incredible observations and insight divulged in this book will shine a new light on any equine experience, whether you are an experienced trainer or going on the donkey trail on the beach.

The Equine Semaphore Code

the horse talks back

by Meljay Turner

www.meljayturner.com

Table of Contents

Introduction

I'd had enough. I threw the whip away. I couldn't hurt this horse any longer.

I had a really special bond with him, but he was a horse with serious behavioural issues. Yet I had the strongest feeling that it wasn't his fault, and that he was, in fact, trying to tell me something. Now, do not get me wrong, I never laid the whip on him, just purely holding the lunge whip in my hand was enough to make all four of his legs go underneath him and defecate in panic.

I have always believed that life is a journey, one that has twists and turns, steep hills and dark tunnels that you can see the light at the end of, but a bottomless pit sits in your way. The journey, though, can create a wealth of knowledge and experience that can last a lifetime, not only for what we do on the journey, but with whose lives we influence on the way. The horses became a big part of this journey in 2012, with more lessons than

I can possibly count.

We would all like to leave a legacy for our children, mine would be:

'Enjoy and experience the journey wherever it takes you. If you fall, then stand up tall. When you are high, remember the little guy!'

But also

Remember the BEAST in you!

I am Beautiful

I am Evolving

I am Achieved

I am Strong

I have a Team

Sometimes we do not always see a Team, but behind the scenes they are always there.

For those with learning disabilities, I hope my quotation helps!

'On paper, a jumble of words. In my head, it has Order, Vision and Passion!'

We cannot always fully get out of our head what we want to explain, the main thing is that it is there in the first place, showing we are always learning and trying to apply.

Also remember the words of Richard Branson 'I

am a dyslexic thinker', then believe you can achieve whatever you choose!

I am a firm believer that there must be a Creator of the universe. Religions have many names for this Creator, and these religions cause so many problems all in the name of a Creator, who is the greatest mathematician.

Others look to the Universe, or just call it Mother Nature, as the power source of all creations. Even those who strongly believe in the evolution theory to the point they have made it their 'belief' or 'religion', cannot deny that the mathematics behind it all is far beyond our small lives to comprehend fully.

Be it a Creator, the Universe or Mother Nature, it has the ability to form and manipulate particles into any shape or form and give it a life source. It is no wonder that the 'little human', who thinks they are so intelligent, still cannot fully understand the workings of life, only theorising and guessing at the many wonders. The result always being, as scripture states, that mankind will never learn the workings of the Creator.

Chapter 1

—

Creating 'The Equine Semaphore Code'

*L*anguage has always fascinated me. Over the years I have studied several: Urdu, Punjabi, French, and German. When my daughter was younger, we even tried making up our own language, called 'Googu', so we could talk to each other in public with no-one else understanding what we were talking about!

Like many things though, that you do not use continually, you can forget. It is the same with any language, the less you use it, the more likely you will lose it. Before using a language however, you need to learn it first!

The biggest misunderstandings come with communication, or miscommunication, and not fully understanding the intentions of the other party. I have struggled with miscommunication with people all my life, especially with back-to-front speaking and inability to get my words out. This meant I ended up isolating myself for a long time. It was not until I tried going to college at the age of forty, that it was pointed out that I had dyslexia, with back-to-front speaking, misunderstanding of the meaning of words and short-term memory issues, you can imagine my relief, I wasn't going mad!

My speech is sometimes forced as I try to connect my brain with my mouth. This means that people sometimes think that I am shouting, but I am not, it just takes effort to form the words, let alone control how they come out of my mouth.

You can say something to me and I will fully understand what you say. Then, if you ask me again in a while, I may have forgotten what was spoken.

It all comes back eventually, with the correct prompt, but I have always had the view of listen well; it must be in there somewhere even if you can't remember it immediately.

If you ask a question and I do not give the right answer, you have asked the wrong question to draw my thoughts out. Which reminds me of the hologram in *I-Robot*, saying to Will Smith 'Ask the right question and I will give you the right answer'.

Disabilities should not be hidden and covered up; they should be accepted and supported, so everyone can have the freedom to express themselves, despite difficulties. However, when it comes to writing a book or blog, it helps to have someone proofread and change the mistakes you might have missed. No one can do all things perfectly, so doing what is your best, must be of value. The aim is to understand the context and keep enjoying what you do.

There is so much support on the internet now for learning disorders; getting a mentor or coach, to help you express yourself, will help you on your way. My advice is do not do it alone when it comes to learning, always aim to reach your highest potential at each given moment. Remember always: progression comes with practice.

When it comes to working with horses, the more I saw people with horse problems, the more I saw there was a miscommunication on both sides: horse and human. The more opinionated a being is, the greater the miscommunication. This has caused some terrible wars through the generations between humans. It is no different when we bring a different species into our lives, especially when we cannot fully understand what they are saying.

In horses, this has led to increased stereotyped behaviour, dangerous behaviour, and so called 'problem' horses. As the price of purchasing a horse has dropped, these problems have risen due new owners of horses not always taking the trouble to get the education and knowledge they need to care for a horse. It is not just low-end purchasers, though, that have issues with horses and we need to understand the horse better to make sure those we domesticate are fully cared for in exchange for their work. It is time to learn its language and bridge the gap of miscommunication.

Studies are on the increase to improve the welfare of horses, looking at ensuring the care of the horses is sustainable and, more importantly, ethical. This is the aim of this book and my long-term research.

It has been long understood that animals will conform to what their owners want. For animals in domestication, it is very difficult for us to see what the true nature of the animal would be. Horses are housed in small stables or fields, completely away from the environment they were designed for.

Training methods involve small-sized work areas, be it a round pen or a rectangle school. Saddles are attached, bits placed in their mouths, shoes placed on their feet and more. What effect are all these things really having on the horse? Is the horse telling us, but we are just not seeing it? Horses are very good at hiding who and what they really are, including the pain they can be in through injury or illness. Therefore, studies are on the increase; to find out more about how these amazing creatures respond to certain things that humans put them through.

Before you say, 'I know my horse' (if you have one, or access to one), you should consider the following:

When you ask a horse to do something new and it flicks its left ear from a forward position along the sagittal line, keeping it upright to a backward position and returning to the forward position, this usually means that the horse is telling you something. In the context here, the sagittal line is a hypothetical horizontal line from the base of one of the horse's ears to the base of the other ear.

In the same scenario; you ask a horse to do something new and it flicks its right ear from a forward position along the sagittal line, keeping it upright to a backward position, then returning to the forward position, what did it say?

Plus, what is a flick of the ear and what is a rotation of the ear? Is there a difference? If so, what do the differences mean and how does the horse use this to communicate its intentions.

When it comes to horses, it has been documented that they use various ear movements and can give communication with those ear movements. We generally see in books that ear movements relate to mood, be it alertness, anger or resting.

However, in my research with the herd at the sanctuary and other horses with behaviour issues that I have worked with, I have found that this is the minimal of what they are communicating. This is not only between themselves, but also with other species of animals and us humans.

Studies are probing deeper into the facial expressions of horses. Those of us who spend lots of time with our horses will already know the facial expressions they pull when we are with them. What though, if there was something about the way that horses communicate, which could be translated into an understandable language that anyone could learn, and implement to their horse?

This became my aim in 2011 when a horse at a riding stables, which my daughter used, started to communicate with me, quite unexpectedly. The more I looked at and watched this horse, the clearer it became that he was trying to communicate with me through his facial expressions.

I love languages, they have always fascinated me, so I learnt the basics of several languages over the years. Now I realised I had a horse who was clearly trying to tell me something! My attention was caught and I found myself drawn into learning another language: this time it was the equine language.

We know that if our horse is across the far side of the field, when we arrive, we can call out its name and it will come over to us. However, what if we knew the 'call' the horse would give to bring the herd running to them? To enter a field and give a loud neigh to say, 'I'm here', 'Where are you?', 'I've missed you' or 'Come to me'. I can hear some of you say, 'She's lost it!', but consider how we expect the horse to learn our language 'Woah',

'Walk on', 'Canter' and so forth.

More studies are looking at using symbols to teach to horses, so they can communicate their preference. We expect the horse to learn anything human that we want it to learn for whatever purpose we want. All this is showing us, however, is that horses have a vast capability to learn, not just words, but also images, movements, tricks and so on. On top of that being able to communicate using symbols shows they have clear cognitive thinking to be able to use these human things we teach them, to communicate back to us.

Am I missing something here? Humans consider themselves the more intelligent beings because we are inventive in a myriad of ways, can put pen to paper and create many scientific things; be it the atom bomb that could kill all life or a lifesaving inflatable devise to prevent us drowning. Here we feel we are clever in teaching the horse to do so many things from tricks, to specialised training moves such as piaffe (this is a horse manoeuvre) by learning our requests, but we have not taken the time to learn their language.

We have not taken the time to look deeper in how they communicate beyond what is already known such as the ears back means they are angry, or the ears are forward it means they are alert.

When I say we have not looked deeper, I am not speaking of ones who have come to have an understanding with their horse or horses, but from a scientific point of view as an intelligent human race, pen has not been put to paper to define all the actions and communication systems that horses use.

This book is looking at changing that. It is time that we looked at what the horses, and indeed animals, are having to say. They have survived this earth longer than us, be it whether you believe in evolution or creation, the animals were here first.

Let us turn the tables and learn what the horse is saying, what does it mean when their ears flick or was it a rotation? Is it only because they have heard something? Or are the ears pointing to where the eyes are looking? Common interpretations in the horse world seem to be missing the bigger picture, and it is this bigger picture that became a focus for me when a horse started to catch my attention because he needed to say something.

We then come to the sounds of the horse, in which more and more studies are starting to record the frequencies a horse emits, however they do not include the meaning of the frequencies of the sounds, just observations that they are different.

Differences in sound would signify something if connected with humans, as language, so why is the human animal ignoring the fact that the horse animal makes all these sounds and they have real meaning? In learning these meanings we could come to a greater understanding of the horse and its needs.

In 2012 my daughter and I obtained a pony, a scrawny wreck of a pony to be precise, but something about him just said 'look after me'. This led to my personal studies of looking deeper into what the horse is trying to communicate. More rescue horses came to us and the start of the sanctuary began. Initially we operated as a non-profit organisation, but for some reason, whilst they were in a state of needing help the funds came in, but once we had rehabilitated the horses the money stopped coming in because they looked well, as if in the minds of those donating that financial help was no longer required. So, we ceased operating as a non-profit organisation and support the horses ourselves. This book contributes to the expenses of caring for the horses.

Initially my observations at this point were to do with the different types of blinks the horse did and at the times they did them. A definite blink once seemed to indicate the word 'Yes', so I started asking the horses simple questions, 'Are you all right?', 'Are you hungry?' and 'Are you cold?'. The horses would either give a constant stare or blank face, or they would give a definite single full blink. This opens two avenues of thought; first, that horses do want to communicate with us; second, that horses understand human language more than we could possibly imagine. I do not mean the technology side, but the basics of general daily needs and requirements.

I started putting this to the test, by being specific with what I asked, looking for the obvious signs that I had now started to learn. This was the start of creating a new ethogram: the dissertation I produced at university had an ethogram in it with precise measurements and actions. From there it has increased to the ears, tongue and the connection between the facial expressions and the movements on the body and how all of these, when put together, create a language.

Just observation was not enough, video footage

of horses' behaviour together in a herd and the herd of horses I work with started to grow. By accident, however I do not believe in accidents as all things must happen for a reason, I thought I saw something when watching back one of the videos, but the quality of the video makes it too quick to identify on normal speed, so I slowed the video down.

I was amazed at the precise lip actions and tongue actions two horses had displayed between each other, that if I had not known how to lip read and use some sign language, I would have missed it. The lip speech between the horses was ordered and showed a conversation, one thing was lacking. I had not learnt their language yet, so I didn't have a clue what they had said.

I started to live out with the herd as much as possible, they started to accept me as part of them. Having an understanding how the lead mare operates, I followed that lead and established my role within the herd while I was there.

When that role was understood, the horses started to be more open with their communication and I started to see more and more of the lip speech conversation they had between each other.

One day the lip speech was obvious between

two of the horses, which changed my perspective on the hierarchy ranking of horses as it was understood. The quiet gelding, a ten-hand high Chestnut Shetland Pony, Barney, was in the carrel eating with the main herd and I had, what I call the 'protector' of the herd, Pye, near me.

Pye is the bossy one of the herd and the one that will fight first when new comers enter the herd, currently understood in the equine world as the hierarchy. He was on watch duty while the others ate and the Shetland pony Barney turned around from eating and started the lip speech movements, Pye turned and watched and then responded with lip speech back to Barney.

I gave the expression of questioning Pye what was said, Pye promptly turned around and demonstrated; moving all the herd away from the hay except for... Barney. Barney turned back to where he was and carried on grazing all on his own. Pye then positioned himself between Barney and the rest of the herd, leaving Barney with all the hay to himself.

This was the first time I had seen Pye respond to something Barney had asked, which, to me, demonstrated that there was an order system that put Barney as the hierarchy and not the bossy Pye.

Pye turns out to be the protector of the hierarchy gelding and mare. This may also explain in studies why some stallions allow other stallions to be within the herd, it is a protective role of those taking the lead. It has been fascinating to watch this in detail over the years.

In 2016 I went to university, even though it has been a big gap since I left school with just CSEs in 1984. My chosen course was a BSc in Equine Sports Therapy and Rehabilitation. Not only did going into mainstream education show up why I struggled so much at school with writing, with dyslexia being diagnosed only when I was forty years old, but also a higher form of autism that in group scenarios completely blew my mind away; panic attacks, meltdowns, and big explosions in the classroom for tutors saying silly little things like 'It's easy really!' I must laugh that I can understand a communication system between the horses, yet when it comes to a 'simple' figure to work out a maths sum on paper, I have a meltdown. Give me a spreadsheet every time with codes and I will be happy. It made me re-evaluate the journey of my life I had already gone through and focus more on where I want to go.

Being in an equine university environment was distressing in many ways, not only from my dyslexia aspect, but also from understanding what the horses were communicating. I was five years into my learning and understanding the equine communication system when I started university and seeing the horses' frustration being in confinement most of their time, and much more, was all clearly identified to me by what the horses had taught me.

They were identifying their pains to me, but I was unable to help because of rules and regulations, and others not understanding that the horse had just told me something.

It was clear as I observed people around the horses that they do not understand the equine language, with only minimal understanding of the meanings of the ear actions; 'ears pinned back equals aggressive' and 'ears forward means alert', etc. There is so much more that has not been documented, not only in studies, but also books that just keep repeating the same old things over and over.

How could I possibly get the message over that horses have a language that human beings can (and should) not only learn, but also use in communicating back with the horses?

The more I read journals and books it became clear that I was not the only one looking, in more depth, at the communication system of the horses. Studies focused on facial expressions, be it horses pulling expressions or horses recognising our facial expression.

These studies looked at how they reacted to things that humans did and so forth, but it was all still restricted and as I read and continue to read the journals and books the capacity of what they found were minimal. Watching the appendix video footage of experiments showed so much of what they were missing while trying to identify their hypothesis. It became clear to me that they did not have a baseline to work from, without a baseline, nothing can be understood.

The focus of my personal study became the ears, and the more time I spent out with the horses, observing them, it was clear that the ears were not just an indicator of mood, but also a signal to others of the direction they were going to take. This all made sense, how can horses galloping across the plains or waters know exactly what each one is going to do, or where they will go, to prevent accidents. I started watching YouTube videos of horses, falls, bolting, jumping, or refusing to jump and it was so clear that the ears said it all! But that was not all, when new horses I met realised I had just said 'Hello', or acknowledged them in their language, their ears started moving all over the place in patterns that I could recognise, but I had no understanding of the meaning. I would respond in their way I did not understand, and they again responded that they understood.

How do I move forward now, to show that horses want to communicate and create a system that is able to be learnt? A book is just a book without science to back it up, so I needed to find out how to make that science. It was during the last part of my first year at university that gave me the answer, but I nearly quit before then.

At nearly fifty years of age I knew I was not cut out for higher education, it's not my aspect of learning. I have always learnt best in my own ways, in fact, the first semester at university it was about what type of learner are you, with the traditional four suggestions of; visual, auditory, reading/writing and kinesthetic, but none of these seemed to fit me fully.

Finally, I found other methods of learning and

one that fitted me - solitary learner. However, being a solitary learner meant I could not put to paper what my tutors wanted to see in assignments and exams. I was even worse at remembering the information they wanted me to learn for exams, without prompting.

I had a meeting with the head of equine and year tutor and it was suggested I had a year gap and came back to it, but I knew if I did, I wouldn't go back. I am glad I kept going despite how difficult it became for me.

My dissertation had to be the way forward, but how? I asked if I could use something connected with my horse whispering experience and it was agreed I could look at the equine language, after all language is science.

When I submitted my first proposal to the dissertation board, I was informed it was big enough to be a PhD and was told I had to reduce it down. I had only chosen two aspects of the ear movements, but the activities connected with it would have been too much data. Reducing the dissertation down in the final year to just one ear action – the 'at rest' or 'neutral' position, as most horse people know it as. In the study by Waltham et al., (2015), it was stated that the 'neutral' ear position, which can be seen when a horse is at rest, is not always consistent and there are variations of the position. That was my topic, the variations of the ear positions at rest. There is a reason for this and, as my book goes on to reveal, that this ear position is not only used in the 'at rest' position but used in other areas of the horse's communication.

There was another problem after writing my literature review; how to measure the data. Collecting the data and starting to sort it I was, once again, told I have too many variables with the code system I had created and had to reduce this down, again! This opened my eyes to why no-one else has gone this deep before, the restriction of what is expected is so tiny that it would take years at this pace to achieve anything in documentation.

The only time that a consistent ear position is used at rest is when the horse is at rest either when on its own, or in a herd where the spaces between the horses are far enough away from each other. But first I had to identify the 'at rest' ear position, as everyone seemed to have a different idea as to where that position was or mentioned variations of it. Again, there is a reason for this and it relates to how horses communicate.

A person who might have their horses in a stable will see it resting with an ear position that is different to that of a horse that is resting on its own in a field and, again, if resting in a herd. Each position has a different meaning, this also reveals something about the horse and its comprehension of its environment.

It was observing only that one position that led me to realising that it could mean multiple things; 'I am standing', 'I am slowing', 'I am stopping', 'I am adjusting speed'. What I was observing among the free moving herd at the sanctuary needed to be put to the test fully. I couldn't have been the only person with this opinion, there had to be a way to document this scientifically, which I did for my dissertation.

During the study however, I collected the data I needed to show that horses do not just use their ears for listening, but they use their ears to communicate the direction they are going to take. Even more so, that they use their ears to chat to each other in a form of code which reminded me of the Maritime Semaphore Code, hence the title of the dissertation was - *The Equine Semaphore Code (TESC) – An ethogram of the horses' ear movements.*

Part one involved identifying the 'at rest' ear position in other areas of the horse's activity. This led to me deepening my understanding, looking at things from a different point of view and putting in writing what I am sure many people already know, but it has yet to be documented. One thing I learnt at university: if it has not been critically reviewed, it is just an opinion.

After a second reduction and a third submittal of my proposal a problem arose yet again... I had to reduce my study even further! This also meant changing the title of the study and the hypothesis.

I insisted that the code that I had created remained in the study, but all I could do was create a tally from the code using the lateral point of view of the different ear positions of horses resting. This proves nothing except horses can move their ears, which is disappointing, or so I thought.

The new title of the dissertation was now - "The Equine Semaphore Code (TESC) – An ethogram of horses' ear movements". Part One: "Identifying the variations of the 'at rest' ear position".

In university seeing the horses contained, most of the time with crowds of students around them, I saw the horses' continual communication with each other from the stalls, over the tops of the heads of the students. It was amazing to watch, with the students and staff being completely oblivious to the conversations happening between the horses.

Unfortunately, there was also a downside, the horses did not like the confinement or the way they were being used. The worst expression I struggle with is a horse saying, 'Help me'. You already know that expression in humans. We see it on the appeal advertisements around Christmas, of children struggling and that look on their faces that says, 'Help me', it is the same with the horses. Studies have already identified the equine 'pain face' in both ridden and non-ridden scenarios, and it is clear to see if you know what you are looking for.

One day in university, during a lesson, students put paint on a horse to show where the muscles were.

The horse had stood patiently for the painting and gave no indication that it was stressful for him, but when it came to washing off the paint, with seven students all around him scrubbing in every direction and cleaning him, he could not cope.

I had been standing too long already, having

lower back issues and I was in pain, so I was standing outside the pen while they washed him.

With so many hands scrubbing him all over, he, not surprisingly, started to become stressed and fidgety. Because of this, they then held his head collar to keep him still, to finish cleaning him. Still fidgeting, he looked over the students' heads directly at me and gave the 'Help me' look. (The layout was a rectangle pen, the horse and students were inside the pen and I was outside it watching) I just wanted to cry knowing I had no power to intervene with what was happening, all I could relay back to the horse was 'I'm sorry' and I could feel the tears welling up inside me.

No-one could see the emotional distress that the actions around him were causing, even as they were holding him to make him stand still. That was not the only occasion that the horses said, 'Help me'. Although the memory of those faces sticks in my mind, I record everything to aid my dyslexia for the written side of the work and I have those images captured also on video, which give me a greater reason to define the language of the horse.

Why should we, the intelligent race, be so narrow- minded when it comes to realising that animals communicate with us - or at least want to - on a much greater scale than just saying, in effect, 'Feed me'.

It is not just the ears that are used to communicate. Facial expressions, movement of the tongue, the lips and movement of the eyes all pointed to communication between the horses. The more I watched, without intervening with the horses, the more I saw. From being a part of our herd, including stopping out overnight with them, the more I came to understand.

One thing I noticed on the videos from university was that, during handling, the handlers rarely looked at the horses' faces. It hit me; how could they possibly know what the horses are saying if they never look at the faces? It is the first port of any conversation.

The hours of video recordings of the sanctuary horses and others that I worked with, brought to light the speed at which horses communicate. Our lips move fast with our speech, but horses' can communicate even faster when connecting all of their actions together.

Ears, eyes, mouth, tongue, nose, head, body, legs, and tail, move in unison with each other to create a discernible language and one which we can interpret and use in return to communicate with the horse. Books always seem to pick up on a couple of actions, but it is time we started putting all these actions together.

A new coding system has been created and is detailed later in the book, with the aim of connecting the variations. The coding system, as I've said, has been named *The Equine Semaphore Code (TESC)*.

Let's start looking…

'Humans take the time to learn an established language that exists among the animal species, breaking the barrier of communication between the human and non-human animal'.

As a global species, we human beings pride ourselves on being the greater thinking beings, understanding binary, radio waves and creating more and more technology, to aim and advance the human race. But we often lack the ability to see what is right in front of us; a simple repetitive language that we can learn.

This language is the language of the horse, you will find that most animals have some kind of language, but for this book we focus on the horse.

The horse: a species that is so willing, touchingly willing if you think about it, to do things for us. It learns what we want it to learn, be it they are handled with care or through violence and inflicted pain. We owe it to them to learn to understand them better.

This book is *not* about telepathic communication with horses. My focus is the visible language that exists in the animal kingdom, in which our domesticated friends are already using to communicate with us, but we fail to understand.

Let us see where the twenty-first Century takes us!

Chapter 2

—

Who Am I?

*T*his is such an interesting question that we all ask ourselves over time. 'Who am I?' It was a question I asked myself for a long time, after reading a poem from a dear neighbour with that very title 'Who am I?' It was a sad, deeply moving poem from a woman whose life had brought her down to the bottom of a pit, but within that pit there was beauty. I read that poem, but was made to promise never to share it, so I haven't. I lost contact with that neighbour, but I hope that the beauty she saw in the bottom of the pit comes out fully in her life.

So, who am I? It is a question that can change daily, weekly, and so on, because everything we do in life creates who we are inside. As a child I was quiet and shy, I did not start speaking fully until I was three years old. In my teens I was an enthusiastic footballer, being one of the only girls allowed to play on the five-aside boys' teams. This was the days that girls playing football was not lady like!

In my twenties I had two children, a messy divorce and lost custody of my children to my ex-husband's parents. That really changed who I was inside. I was going to write in more detail about this, but the more I remembered, the more the pain in my heart grew and I had to stop thinking about it.

A second marriage, another child and another divorce all changed me again. Disabilities and ill health made more changes. Work, university, friends and so on all made a difference.

One factor that never changes though, or at least I take stringent efforts to make sure it doesn't change, is the kindness in my heart, which I hope is clear to everyone I meet.

I'm a dyslexic thinker, which makes me seem nutty at times, however, that also makes it possible for me to see things from a different angle. If I had not been dyslexic, I ask myself, 'Would I have seen what I see in our equine friends?''. Angles are the key to unlocking the coding system that the horses have within their communication system. Along the way I used this understanding of the horse's communication system and acquired the nickname the Horse Talker, rather than the Horse Whisperer.

After my presentation at Hartbury University, for *The Equine Semaphore Code*, things went a little bit mad for a couple of weeks. The overload of doing everything, at home, for our herd and travelling over one-hundred and twenty miles a day for university three days a week, sent me off into a meltdown that made me stop and reflect, but not as expected. I went on a long slow walk through the night for about ten hours and ended up in the hospital care unit under section two of the Mental Health Act. Just what I needed to separate from the hectic three years of university, working or trying to work to live, writing this book, building the sanctuary, looking after a daughter with social anxieties and my older daughter's partner in hospital having a kidney transplant. For the two weeks I was in care, I was able to fully refocus on what mattered most.

This time, putting myself first, I started a jiggy dance-walk to try and get fitter. Helped by the support of the Darren Hardy team online I took up the #ravenrun 90 day challenge and took on hashtag #dancewalk. I still could not walk fully without enormous amounts of pain, but jigging meant I could get that bit further. An inspiring story, just Google search #ravenrun and #dancewalk together. An inspiring story of will with Robert Raven Kraft, aka #Raven.

Life is a journey that takes us down the paths that we need so that we can grow. Every moment in life has a lesson to teach if you are open to it. After *The Equine Semaphore Code* the next step in my journey will be all about 'My Journey', to who I have become, in *'Raven, Daily and Dark Horse - Living on the wrong train track'*. Keep your eye out for its release.

Chapter 3

—

Horses' Ears and Commonly Understood Meanings

C ommon body language and signs recognised in horses in general from information that is taught within colleges and riding schools is relatively basic; when a horse has its ears pinned back, the horse is angry, and it might bite or kick.

When the horse is at rest, the ears are back and relaxed. If it is feeling unwell, its ears rest loping outwards. This could be expanded if the meaning of what the horse is communicating through its ears could be understood in greater detail.

I had thought to quote sections of literature from the one hundred and twenty journals that I studied for my research. However, they are one and the same. All that they study are specific movements, or series of movements, with no real conclusion other than 'Horses can move their ears'. The more I read, the more bored I became. In all of the time we have studied and documented horse behaviour nothing has changed, it is only reiteration of pre-existing publications, with no expansion in understanding of what this could mean.

My studies have shown different variations of ear positions beyond that of what is already taught in mainstream equestrian schools. I have found through my research that it is not *only* the angle at which a horse holds its ear(s), that expresses communication, but also the way the ear changes position, whether it is a flick or a rotation; each movement and angle holds different meaning. A flick is where the horse's ear remains in an upright position while moving back and forth, which was mentioned in Chapter 1, and a rotation would be where the horse's ear might be in an alert forward position but move down and out to a backward angry position in a single movement.

Part of my research has been observing the best and worst horsemanship methods. We know that training the horses can be achieved using any method due to the compliance of the horse, be it a round pen, square pen, riding school or an open field.

Understanding what the horse says to us, however, is a whole new picture. Footage watched of trainers shows they are still not seeing what is being communicated and it is completely missed by the handler, with trainers fixed on what they want to make the horse to do. I have been at fault with this many times and, on watching my own video footage back, I can see I have missed things. Stepping back from that has allowed me to see what the horse is saying, it has been an interesting and enlightening path.

What ear positions do you know and what meaning do you understand them to have?

Got questions about your horse, or the book?
Please submit at www.meljayturner.com

Chapter 4

—

Visual Signs

*E*very horse's head is different, just as people's heads are all different, including siblings that are born with identical DNA; there are still differences in appearance and behaviours. In a horse, every ear position sits slightly differently on the head, every horse's ear shape is indeed slightly different. It is the same with the human body composition, each of these differences make identification of each other possible.

It is true that, to the untrained human eye, horses might look much the same and we might not notice the many different angles and positions horses' ear holds. Ears are generally described as 'backward' or 'forward', but with so many variations the question I kept asking myself was 'How are they forward?' and 'How are they backward?'. With all the variations I've seen in studies, that all describe multiple positions in the same way, what makes the differences and what meaning do they have?

One element of my research was to show that horses do not use their ears as part of saying where their attention is, as perceived in many studies. A good example of this is asking the horse to stand still at liberty, with no other horses around them, then steadily walk all the way around the horse with the video recording.

In the screen grabs from the video, this gave the footage of exactly where the horse's ears are positioned at several angles while they are stationary, which helped in defining the ethogram. It also showed that his eyes clearly followed me, which changed the shape of the eye. He was focused on me, but his ears did not follow me, which disproved the idea that where the ears are pointing to is where its attention is.

I did this with the horses, time after time, and the results were the same. Asking the horse to 'stand' while I walked around them, they would comply with their ears in this relative position.

What is clear from the photographs acquired is that the apex of the ear is visible in almost every circumstance the horse finds itself in. This would point to the communication side of the ears being focused on the apex of the ears.

Comparing a horse that is heavily sedated and standing still shows different ear positions to that of a horse that is not under sedation and asked to stand still. To calculate this the angle of the ears can be determined by the set markers, like anything if you do not have set markers for measuring, you cannot measure it. There is more about this in Chapter 7 where I define the ethogram, explaining *The Equine Semaphore Code (TESC)* and how it works.

What ear positions have you noted that are different from the commonly understood meanings? Are any of those ear positions repetitive? What is occurring in the environment around the horse that may have an influence on the horse's behaviour?

Got questions about your horse, or the book?
Please submit at www.meljayturner.com

Chapter 5

—

Defining Language

*B*efore I go further, consideration is needed for what language is and my reason for being precise about this. It is regarded as a uniquely human invention, one that has evolved over time and which is, above all, expressed in speech, where language uses a system of essential arbitrary sounds arranged in a highly systematic way, to allow human beings communicate. I must disagree with this. From my learning, the animals already have an elaborate speech system that has been overlooked.

Many languages, though not all, can be written down. It is important to acknowledge that language, which is probably coeval with human evolution, was spoken for many millennia before it was written down; written language has only existed for about 6,000 years, if you base it on bible chronology.

There are specialised forms of language, of course. For those hard of hearing, sign language is a genuine and recognised form of language.

Other areas that are considered as language are that of computers. One specialised form of language, very relevant to this book, is the Marine Semaphore Code formerly used on warships and sometime used even today on ships, when modern electronic communications are not available. Human language is quite rightly considered an essential resource of our species, and essential for normal life.

In more recent years it has been noted that animals have a communication system too. Cats and dogs have been noted to be able to communicate and understand human communication.

With studies now starting to look at how horses use their communication system, it has been identified that they have seventeen facial expressions and more tongue actions have been defined connected with enjoyment. In dogs, the tongue hanging out of the side of the mouth has been related to happiness, is this something that we can also connect to horses?

Without further studies that operate with a baseline, it is still all guess work, making this book a baseline for deeper studies into the animal communication system.

Have you been in a situation where you felt a horse was trying to communicate something to you that is not commonly taught? What was the horse doing and what was occurring in the environment around the horse?

Got questions about your horse, or the book?
Please submit at www.meljayturner.com

Chapter 6

—

Finding the Equine
Ear Muscles

Finding information in books or online journals about equine ear muscles is surprisingly difficult. There is plenty of information on the position of horses' ears and the internal workings of the horses' ears, but hardly anything on the muscles and how the ear muscles function. Some sources claim that there are just eight muscles to move the horses' ears, others that there are ten muscles and some twenty-three. I even had our university librarian look for me and he was shocked at how little information about horses' ear muscles was available.

Even the question of how many ear muscles there are is still an unanswered question; essentially, you need to consult several sources and try to evolve your own view of which sources to trust. In fact, it was in a Pinterest post, I found what seemed to be someone's college work showing the structure of the muscles behind the horses' ears and a book that showed the muscles, but even then, other journals had added additional muscles or changed the names of muscles that the older books had detailed.

However, none of the books and journals had complete details, mainly due to the connection of their reason for writing, such as injuries or illnesses connected to the inner ear or one study of an ear that had been torn half off and needed sewing it back together.

Each new publication seemingly found another muscle that the previous investigations missed out. When in touch over Facebook with a lady who specialises in dissection, I was told that the horses that are provided for tests have already been skinned and most of the time the ears have been removed or the head cut off, damaging that area of the muscles.

It would be good to see a full dissection based not just on photos of the muscles, but actions that each of the muscles perform, and how each action of the individual muscles changes the action of another individual muscle. If the zygomaticoscutalaris is active, how does this affect the scutuloauriculartis profundus, or interscutularis? How many muscles does it take for the horse to turn its ear backward laterally and how many muscles does it take to turn the ear backward in an upright position? At this point, my brain has constructed a dissection and is experimenting by pulling muscles around to see how they all interact with each other.

Individually, we can define the direction the muscles can contract, which on its own would generate a specific movement. However, horses do not use isolated individual muscles to move their ears and a dissection would be required to see the full movement of the horse's ears and how each the muscles move as groups.

With around ten muscles moving each ear pinna, this gives great scope for a variety of movements and positions that have still yet to be recorded or investigated in journals.

If the muscle cervico-auricular profundus major moved just one millimeter, and no other ear muscles, what position would this place the horse's ear? If the cervico-auricular profundus major contracted one millimeter along with the cervico-auricularis superficialis, how would that affect the angle of the pinna? If drinking water had an involuntary action on the horses' ears, which I confirmed it did in my dissertations, what other pressures applied would affect the actions of the ears? Bridals, either bitted or bitless, head collars, a dually (a proprietary horse training device) and rope holsters all tend to sit across the muscles over the top of the head that are connected to the horses' ears, even when fit fitted correctly. How does it affect the freedom of the movement of the horses' ears? Further research into the equine ear muscles would be required to answer these questions.

If the horse is using their ears to communicate, are the tools we use preventing this from happening and does it matter? During my research looking at head positions of the horse, especially when human pressure applied using bridals, head collars, dually, rope halters and any man-made control device to the head, the previous studies neglected to include what impact this was having on the horse's ability to move its ears freely, as part of its communication system.

Some riders wonder why the horse's ears become floppy when riding with the horse's head in a certain position, where the chin is flexed towards the chest, such as in dressage performances. Neither my research, nor the journals I have studied, have taken in to account the way bridals etc. inhibit the horse's ability to be able to use the ears in a natural manner.

I remember one of my tutors saying, at university, that no one takes any interest in the horses' ears as "There is no money in the ears". This is most likely the reason why no one has taken studies into equine communication further – money. Humans are only generally interested in something if they can make money out of it. Please note I said "generally", I know that does not apply to everyone!

What tools or aids do you use and how do you think they may impact a horse's ability to communicate intentionally with their ears?

Got questions about your horse, or the book?
Please submit at www.meljayturner.com

Chapter 7

—

The Equine Semaphore Code: TESC - The Code

*T*he code is not complete in this book, and whilst I am writing this, my head is telling me so much more that I wanted to detail, but writing it in a way in which everyone will understand cannot be done in just one book. So, the details I have placed for you in this book only touch the surface of my research. Having now spent over 10,000 hours' worth of studying the equine language, since 2011, no book can hold all the information and learning I possess. This book, though, does give the starting point of a method of measuring what we are seeing in the horses' ears.

The Figures that you will need for this next part are *The Equine Semaphore Code* both lateral (1a) and frontal views (1b).

The BSc dissertation was very limiting in terms of what could be documented, I always had too many variables and had to keep refining my dissertation. The final information collected for the dissertation was just footage of the horses at rest and counting the various ear position, assigning *The Equine Semaphore Code* to each of these actions and looking at any possible visible movements from the horses that could have instigated the variations, with the results being quite conclusive.

Throughout my personal studies and data collected for the dissertation, I identified from either a frontal view (Figure 1b) or lateral view (Figure 1a). These figures identify the sagittal plane that the ears are sitting, assigning a code to each sagittal line in roman numerals (i) for the upper and (ii) for the lower sagittal line. The upper sagittal line is connected with more alert and general moods, and the lower sagittal line is connected with more expressive moods.

Before the dissertation I had noted nineteen different lateral ear positions, this can be seen in the Figure 1a, be it the horse's ears are forward, facing laterally outwards or backward. These positions could be on either sagittal line. So, this had to be the focus during my BSc study, more details about this below. With this baseline I labelled the lateral view in numbers one to nineteen. Nineteen being the ears pinned tight to the neck, 'angry' position, and one, being a position I have only seen in the racehorse industry, pointing horizontally forward at a ten-degree angle.

5
6
7
8
9
10
11
12
13
Left
Angle
50°
60°
70°
80°
90°
80°
70°
60°
50°
Right
Angle
4 — 40°
40° —14
3 — 30°
30° —15
2 — 20°
20° — 16
1 — 10°
10° —17
Sagittal (i)
Line (ii)
0° — 18
-10° —19
Cranial
Lateral nearside

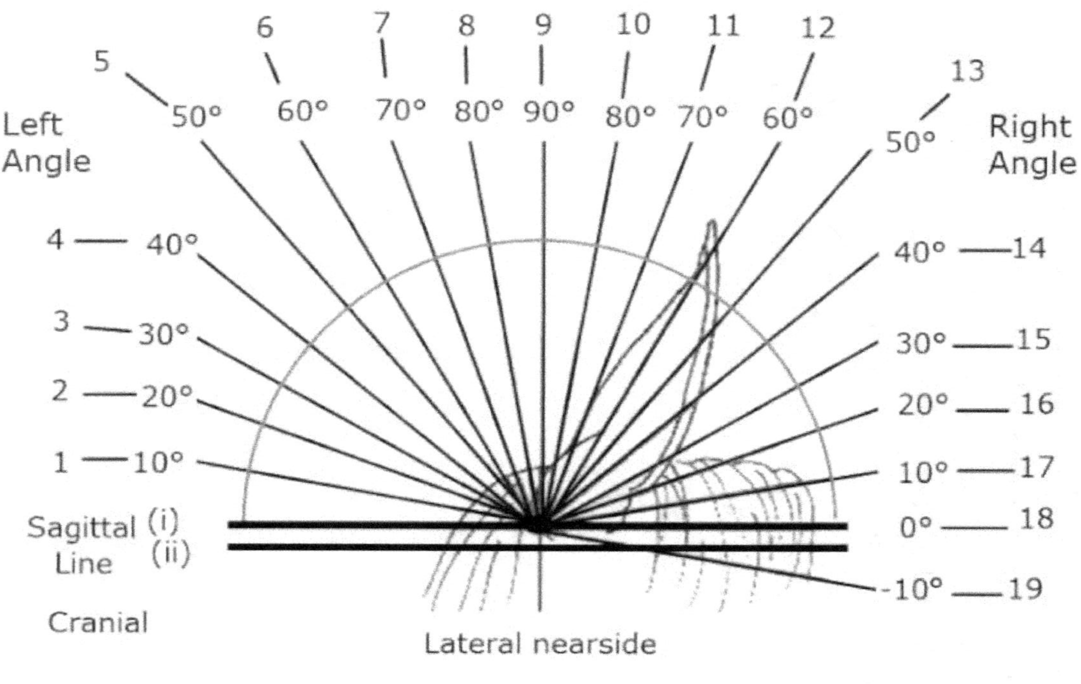

Figure 1a

Nearside
(Right)
Offside
(Left)
C
B
A
A
B
C
60°
70°
80°
90°
80°
70°
60°
D — 50°
50° — D
E — 40°
40° — E
F — 30°
30° — F
G — 20°
20° — G
H — 10°
10° — H
(i)
(ii)
Sagittal Lines
Frontal View

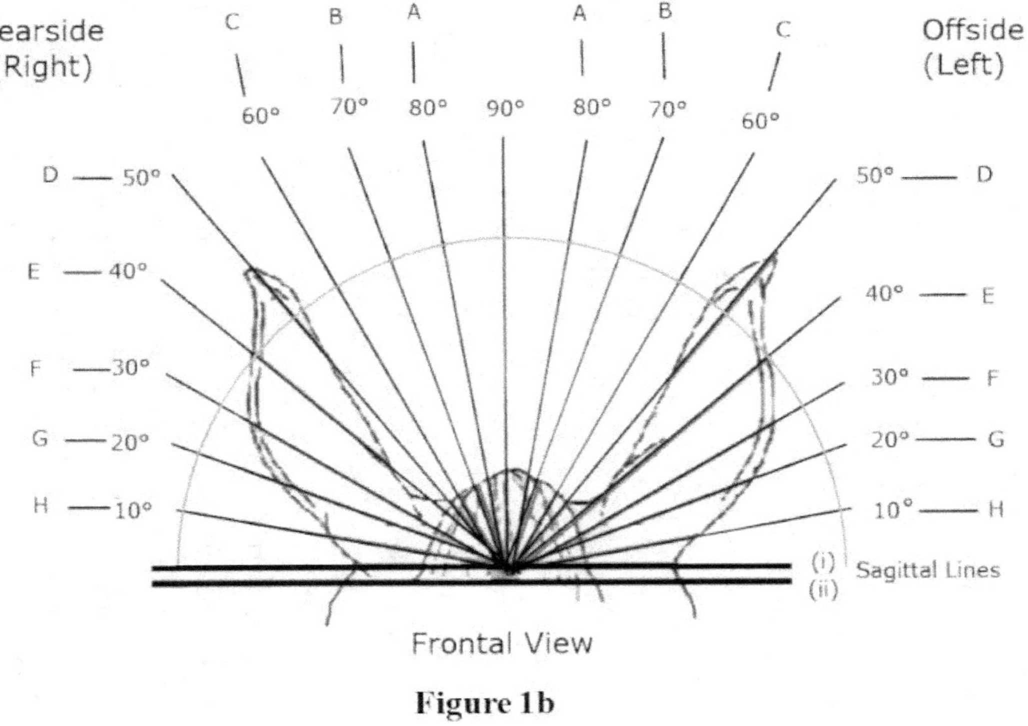

Figure 1b

From a frontal view of the horse, it was identified that the horses would hold their ears in eight various angles; the most upright with the apex of the ear pointing towards the medial plane of eighty-degrees vertically and the furthest horizontal line at an angle of ten-degrees. The frontal view is identified in letters A (most vertical) to H (most horizontal).

Due to each ear being able to move independently of each other, they are labelled in the ethogram individually. Each ear is labelled nearside (NS), the horse's left, and offside (OS), the horse's right.

During the studies the traditionally understood 'at rest' ear position was identified from a frontal view on only one horse, this horse had no other horses nearby, with a clearance of around fifteen feet. With the horses that grouped together the ear position varied depending where the other horses stood around them. It was noted on this video footage that the horses grouped themselves according to colour (Figure 2), despite their breed, so chestnuts together, Skewbalds and Piebalds together, Grey and Palameo Dun together and the Blueroan on his own.

Figure 2

The method behind the research - The Equine Semaphore Code.

The apex of the ear is the clearest part of the pinna that is visible above the poll and can be observed from all perspectives around the horse. The aim was to create a new template for measuring the angles of the ears from both a lateral view and frontal view, in order to ascertain a more accurate position of the ears.

A new method of analysing horses' ears was created based on the position of the apex of the ear. Previous observations in books rely on the complete ear, where the whole ear was measured to determine length of ears. However, the apex of the ear is visible from all angles, hence a new measuring system was designed.

The new code for the horse's ears - '*The Equine Semaphore Code* (TESC)' - is based on the angles of the ears from a lateral and frontal view providing a basis for future studies. Marker points from a frontal view are in line with the sagittal markers for the lateral view, from each side of the head.

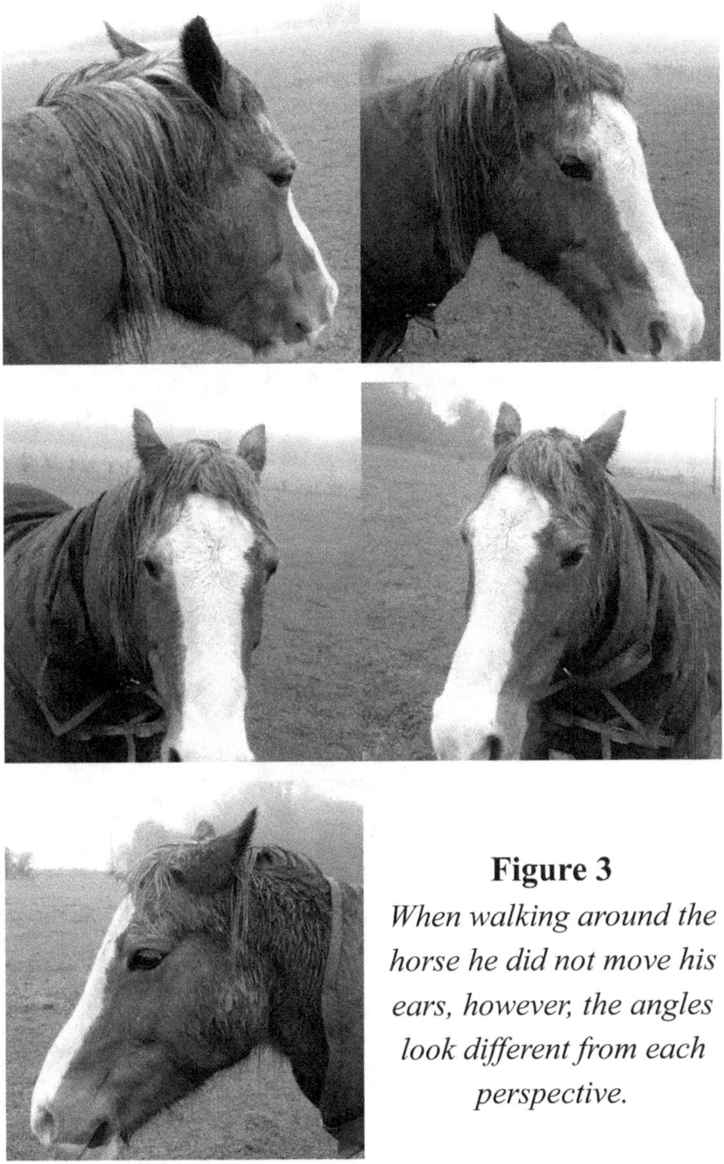

Figure 3

When walking around the horse he did not move his ears, however, the angles look different from each perspective.

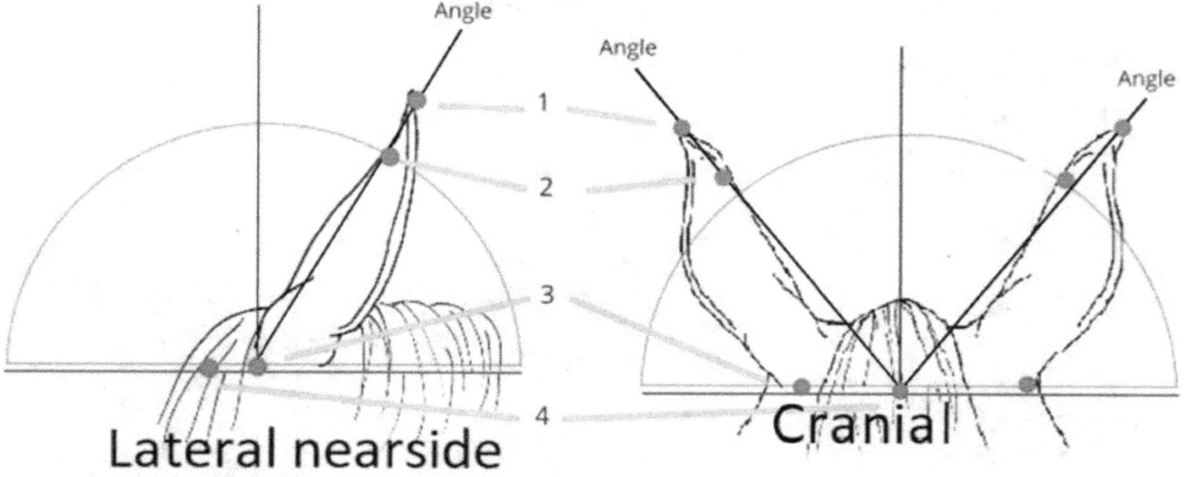

Figure 4

Four marked areas (Figure. 4) demonstrate the marker points that must be used for TESC to function fully - (1) the tip of the apex of the ear, (2) the distal part of the apex of the ear for the guideline to sit on, (3) the base of the ear, and (4) the centre point from a frontal view, connecting the sagittal lines from ear to ear points across the forehead. These marker points are used irrespective of the horse's head neck position, always keeping a horizontal line through the sagittal planes between markers (3) and (4).

Applying the TESC baseline coding system, based on angle increments of ten-degrees from a lateral view and frontal view, collating how many positions were presented. An example of the code in action can be seen, as the horse in this image (Figure 5) became alert to a car driving down the road. Figure 5 identifies the alert ear position, coded as - TESC=(OS(i)8-2(0)). In other words, offside, upper sagittal line, eighty-degrees minus two-degrees cranially, zero signifying that a frontal view was not visible.

The Equine Semaphore Code assigns each ear an identification code, making it trackable digitally; both cranial and laterally; alphabetically from a frontal view along the sagittal line A – H; Roman numerals along the two height levels along the sagittal line at the base of the ears, (i) upper level and (ii) lower level; and numerically for the lateral view one to nineteen.

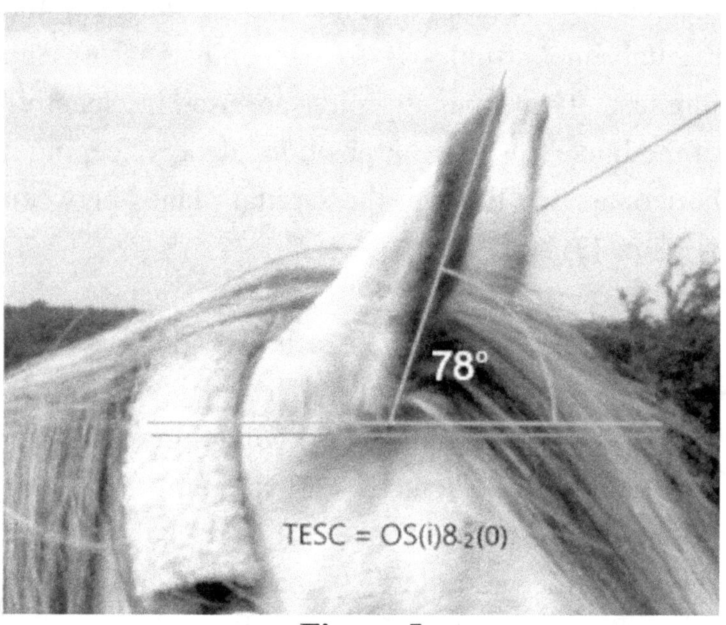

Figure 5

The Equine Semaphore Code Alert Ear Position, lateral view TESC=(OS(i)8-2(0)).

The breakdown of the code, for duplication, can be seen when changing to a new image showing a 'frontal view'. Using the centre point of the horse's face along the sagittal lines, upper or lower, depending on the horse's ear level at the time of measuring.

In Figure 4 the horizontal lines (3) and (4) are identified at the base of the ear from both a lateral aspect and frontal view - (i) upper sagittal line and (ii) lower sagittal line. Identifying where these sagittal lines sit is one of the core markers to distinguish a baseline for calculation of where the horse's ear is sitting, be it they are forward or backward.

These lines to remain horizontal always, irrelevant of the head neck position, between markers (3) and (4); if the horse's head position is in a different angle, to a resting head position, the marker would remain constant.

An example of a horse on the vertical (Figure 6), markers (3) and (4) would not change on the horse's head, however our protractor would.

Figure 6

Head Neck Position (HNP) of a horse being held on the vertical (HNP2), when the image is rotated to the neutral (HNP1) it shows an unnatural ear position.

The only way we can find this out is to measure. My dissertation found that current head neck position calculations had flaws in them as they used three different markers to work them out, based on the withers or jaw or face and they were only suited to one breed type of horse; so, I created a new measurement based on an area that is the same for all horses, the eye. The structure to the skull, that makes the eye socket, has a straight line to the front of the eye. This straight line when measured with a horse's head in a resting position is exactly at a ninety-degree angle vertically, this will be detailed more later.

When we apply that measurement to this horse, bringing the eye angle back to ninety-degrees, makes (Figure 4) markers (3) and (4) horizontal again. In doing this we see a completely different, if not scary, Figure 6 where the ears are in an unnatural position; out laterally, but leaning slightly back, almost at an 'at rest' ear position but not with-it facing outwards.

In this head position the parotidoauricularis muscle (pronounced parroted-oar-rick-u-laris), which main action is to draw the base of the ear ventrally, would not be able to function. You can see the changes to the parotid gland and the parotidoauricularis muscle being drawn back by the angle the head is held. If the horse was trying to pull its ear ventrally it would not be able, due to the compact area now created in the horse's neck.

If the horse is using its ears as part of its communication, there is no doubt that holding the angle of the head in this manner restricts the natural use of the horse's ears.

On with how the code works...

The marker points for the frontal view are from each side of the base of the ear, directly on the top part of the scutiform cartilage, going through the centre point of the forehead. The vertical line matching the medial plane of the horse's face, straight from the middle of the nose through to the middle of the poll. From the lateral view the vertical ninety-degree angle to the front of the horse's ear is on the top part of the scutiform cartilage.

The code from a frontal view has been measured in graduated angles of ten-degrees and labelled A-H (A=80°, B=70°, C=60°, D=50°, E=40°, F=30°, G=20°, H=10°) for each ear, whether right (OS) or left (NS). Making an offside ear code from the front - 'OS' offside, '(i)' sagittal line, '0' showing no lateral view and '(D)' showing a fifty-degree angle to the side of the horses head. Or for short - TESC=(OS(i)0(D)). Depending on the angle of the ear it varies the (alphabet) code. All these angles have been identified in my studies over the years.

For the lateral view, the graduated degree of angles is labelled as one to nineteen, because in my personal studies I've identified nineteen different lateral ear positions. With ninety-degrees being the switch over point between cranial (1=10°, 2=20°, 3=30°, 4=40°, 5=50°, 6=60°, 7=70°, 8=80°, 9=90°), and caudal (10=80°, 11=70°, 12=60°, 13=50°, 14=40°, 15=30°, 16=20°, 17=10°, 18=0°, 19=-10°). From a lateral view the code would be TESC=(OS(i)5(0)) - 'OS' offside, '(i)' sagittal line, '5' a cranial angle of fifty-degrees cranially, '0' signifying a frontal view is not visible. TESC=(OS(i)13(0)) - 'OS' offside, '(i)' sagittal line, '13' a caudal angle of fifty-degrees, '(0)' with no frontal view, and so forth.

To expand this a little bit more, a horse on high alert the code would be both ears. TESC=(OS/NS(i)9(0)). A horse walking forward with both ears forward, shows code TESC=(OS/NS(i)6(0)). A horse showing interest in an object would show code TESC=(OS/NS(i)5(0)). This is based on my research from the terabytes of video footage collected.

The basis of this angle measuring system is preparing for future studies to obtain a more accurate understanding of the horses' ears and their method of using them to communicate.

To be completely accurate, however, the head

neck position (HNP) format had to be changed to be able to be used across all types of horses, as the current measurements in journals and books did not conform to meet the requirements of every horse. Head Neck Positions (HNP) are detailed in studies, however, there is no constant variable as to the deciding factor of the calculations with three various marker points used. These methods would only be suited to one breed of horse and only if it was fit in structure, and not a stallion with a high crest of neck, or a horse with Equine Metabolic Syndrome and a large crest of neck, or a fat or skinny horse where there is atrophy to the withers and neck.

A consistent measurement or marker had to be found that could be applied to all horse breeds, irrelevant of their sex or health. To ensure TESC to be consistent, a new HNP was devised - *The Equine Semaphore Code* Head Neck Position (TESC/HNP). This new method being based on the angles around the horse's superior lacrimal punctum, with the eye being a constant feature in all horses except where injury, or deformity has occurred. The horse's orbital socket is made up of three bone plates - Frontal bone, zygomatic bone, lacrimal bone which creates a vertical structured line to the fore of the horse's eye. This area of the horse is constant across breeds, making it a suitable marker to measure for the angles of the head.

The Equine Semaphore Code Head Neck Position (TESC/HNP) based on left and right angles with the centre point at the medial corner of the eye. Using a journal identifying a HNP1, it demonstrates that the marker point used for the TESC/HNP has an exact ninety-degree angle to the eye. The white circle maker seen in the Figure defines a dorsal (+) or ventral (-) head movement.

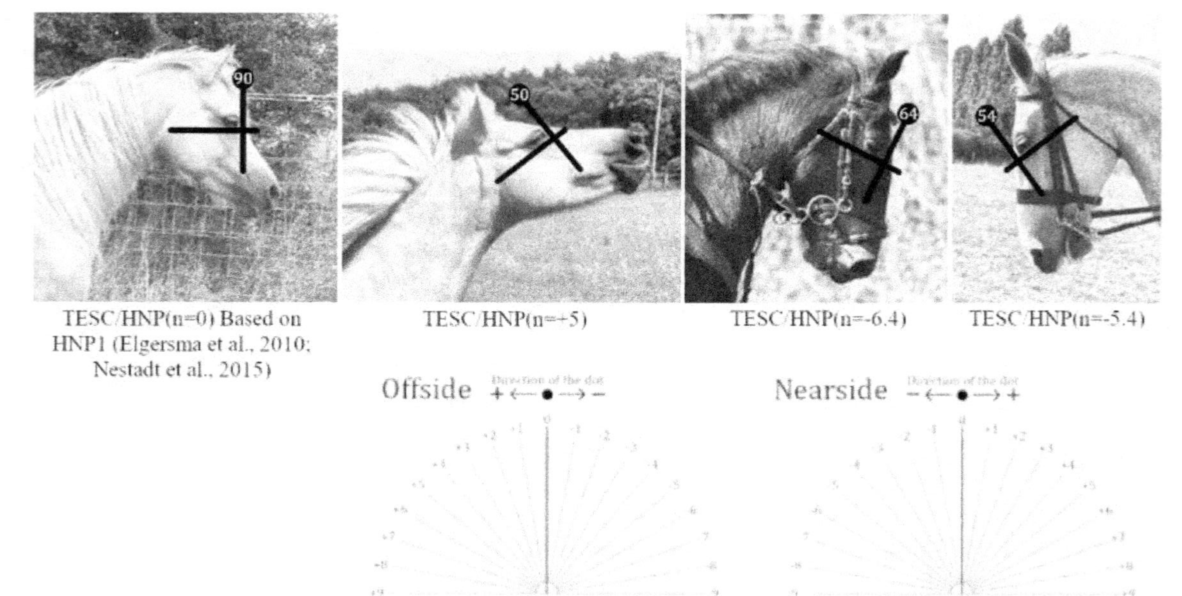

The Equine Semaphore Code Head Neck Position (TESC/HNP)

Figure 7

In layman's terms if the nose goes up, the white circle goes backward and it is a (+), and if the nose goes down the white dot goes forward and it is a (-). Following this bone structure to the eye, this template will fit any horse unless there is deformity to the eye socket.

The original video footage to the dissertation was one hundred and sixty-eight minutes long, but I was only able to use twelve minutes of the horses resting. Observations during the video footage showed the variations of the horses resting ear positions, but also other aspects I had not thought about in the past.

While the horses were drinking, my attention was drawn to the parotidoauricularis, where the origin is the ventral aspect of the auricle and the insertion partially covering the dorsal parotid gland, with insertion to the ventral gland. In Figure 8, showing the position of the parotidoauricularis, it was noted during drinking the ears made a small rotational flick in time with the swallowing action, which may show a greater connection to the muscles in the jaw and throat and involuntary actions of the ears. This is something that I have not yet found in other studies.

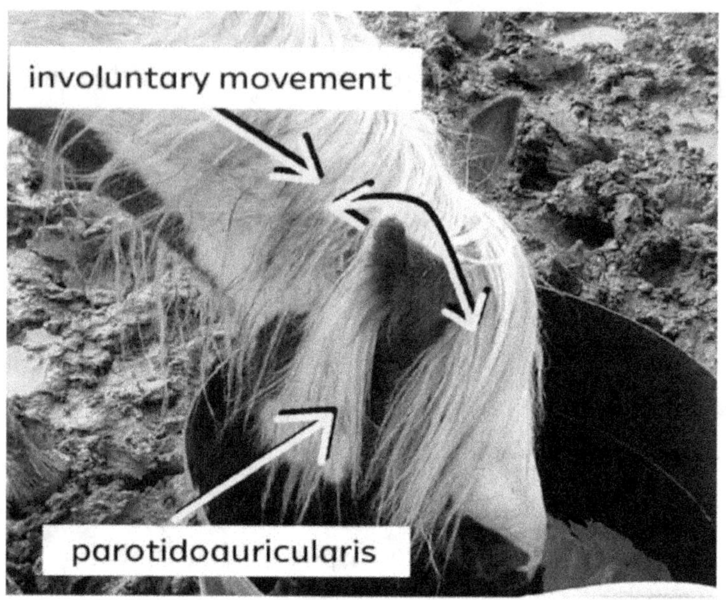

Figure 8

Another area noted during the long-term study and the dissertation footage is the involuntary actions of the ears when shaking their heads after a roll. It is at this point the ears become completely floppy as the head vigorously shakes and all muscle control in the ears ceases.

When you are able to obtain a frontal or lateral image of a horse, using Figures 1a, 1b, 4 and/or 7, what position can you determine the horse's ears are in, relating to the TESC code?

Got questions about your horse, or the book?
Please submit at www.meljayturner.com

Chapter 8

—

How Fast Do Horses Communicate?

Studies have yet to determine how fast a horse sees. It must be faster than a human as it is a flight animal, but the speed at which the horse communicates with each other in relation to human communication, is undetermined and further studies need to be produced.

Logically, the faster an animal moves, the faster it must communicate! We can liken this to us driving a fast car, the faster we go the more aware we become of our surrounding. That is why modern (human) life can be so stressful, despite the technological advancements that are meant to make life easier: the faster people travel and move about, the more data they need to deal with.

Part of my research for this book involves a lot

of slow-motion video footage of horses. In one short video clip I caught on camera with my daughter, who accidentally poked one of the horses in the face with the end of a lunge whip, you see the horse frantically shake his head as he moved away. In slow motion however, it was a completely different story, it detailed the horse making thirteen different facial expressions, within the time frame of my daughter just partly making a surprised look. Those thirteen expressions were made within nine-tenths of a second, including movement of the ears.

Had the footage been viewed only at normal speed, the expressions would not have been visible to the human eye. If horses can produce that many expressions to our one, then the question must be raised as to how fast horses communicate with each other. What might seem just flutters of ears and movements of the head to us, could be a full conversation with another horse. Humans are slow in every aspect when compared to a horse, running, learning, and adapting to new circumstances. Other video footage of the horses in debates with each other are fascinating when watching in slow motion, from eye and lip actions and all connected with feet, tail, and ear actions.

Neither myself nor my tutors at university

found any studies to do with the speed at which horses communicate with each other, which make a very open area that could be considered for further studies.

When observing a slow-motion video of a horse reacting, how many expressions do you see and what do you think they mean?

Got questions about your horse, or the book?
Please submit at www.meljayturner.com

Chapter 9

—

Head Shaking and Nodding

Head shaking has long been connected with horse behaviour issues, which became a focal point of observation during my research. The conclusion that became more evident with observing the herd and then looking at patterns of TV and YouTube footage of horses with head shaking, or nodding, is that it held three areas of communication that has completely been overlooked for the horse. *'I am saying no'* if a horse shakes its head from side to side, the same way we would shake our heads when saying no to something, the horse is doing exactly the same. It is disagreeing with the actions of those around them, be it another horse or a human handler. The more aggressive the head shaking the more the horse is not being listened to and the louder the horse is having to say, *'No'*.

In a herd the horses respect each other, when a horse shakes its head the horse it is communicating to listens and responds within a moment of time. In comparison, when a horse shakes its head, the human does not understand what the horse is saying and carries on with their desired action, trying to convince the horse of what the handler wants, this increases the head shaking of the horse as it continues to communicate its wish not to carry on.

If this is the case, the question is, should the horse have a choice to say, '*No*'? If the horse is really saying, '*No*', are we being morally correct by forcing the horse to continue in something that it is expressing that it does not want to do? For whatever reason it chooses.

Horses use their heads to say, '*Go away*', a nodding action, which I saw occur more on livery yards than it does in a herd. Within the herd I noticed that if a horse went into another's space, and it was not wanted, the horse would nod its head in an upward action, the first movement determining the direction the head is moving. Within a herd, if the opposing horse does not listen, the horse saying '*Go away*' becomes louder. It is no different when a human walks into the space of a horse and the horse does not want it, first there is always the upwards head nodding before the horse takes greater action. Sadly, the horse always getting the blame for misbehaving when it speaks louder.

Another head nodding action is the horse saying, *'Come here'*, where the head nodding action that takes place, it can be a small nod of the head with a downward action of the chin coming to the chest or repetitive if the horse wants something that you have and it is saying, *'Bring it to me'*. A slight downward nod which you must watch closely for, is the horse asking you to come forward into its space. I see this often when meeting new horses and I wait to be invited into their space, never assuming that it is all right just to walk up to them.

Just these three head actions, if understood, could prevent many incidents with horses and their handlers. I have not come across any studies looking at this area of animal communication, if a horse shakes its head it really is saying, *'No'* and *'Stop'*.

Thinking back, in what situations may you have seen a horse saying, '*No*', that has not been seen or understood?

Got questions about your horse, or the book?
Please submit at www.meljayturner.com

Chapter 10

—

The Tongue, the Lips, and the Mouth

*T*he mouth and tongue of the horse play a vital role in their communication system, but it is not always seen in stables unless you know what you are looking for.

The mouth can be observed to move in various speech movements like that of the human animal, it was only by living out with the herd as much as possible, that it was seen between the herd and I called it 'lip speech'. What has been shown as mouth movements in studies, whether independently via horse enthusiasts or scientific studies, it has only been related with calming issues. This is incorrect and only becoming deeply involved with the horses, in a natural environment and with observation only, can these lip movements be understood more. Taking the human element away from studies, a whole new lip speech is observed.

The tongue is an essential part of the horse's communication, from saying in our words '*I like you*', often seen between mares and stallions/geldings, but also shown between same sexes and towards humans. This is a small curling upward tongue action, like us saying the word '*like*' hence the term '*I like you*'.

'*I want food*' is a longer flowing action with a small curl to the end of the tongue as it is extended, several of the herd at the sanctuary would do this while waiting at the gate, near the tack room, when asking for food.

Then we have a very rude '*Go away*' (Figure 9), the latter being seen quite often in livery yard environments, and one we often see in humans a quick sharp protruding tongue action.

A cheeky '*Told-you-so*' action is also detailed as long and protruding, with a downward curl (Figure 10). One of my client's horses, Jenosa, used to do that each time her owner came to visit. She would look over at me and give me that tongue signal as if to say, '*I told you she would come*'. There are many more, but these are the ones that are obvious when in livery yard environments. Observing the herd in their natural environment, I've not fully counted the amount of variations to these actions, many of them connected with lip actions.

Further video footage would be required to determine all of the expressions with the tongue, not only the length the tongue is extended from the mouth, but also the angles at which the tongue curls. Each motion a horse's tongue presents has different meaning. We could never duplicate all the tongue actions a horse can do, but we can learn their interpretation through observation.

Figure 9

'Go away'

Figure 10
'Told-you-so'

What mouth and tongue actions have you observed
from a horse? Are any of these actions repeated?
What do you think they might mean?

Got questions about your horse, or the book?
Please submit at www.meljayturner.com

Chapter 11

—

Eyes and Communicating

Sitting, resting with the herd, the horses in their standing sleep mode, with a still, glazed look in their eyes. I gently leaned towards one of the horses faces, there was no reaction.

I moved a little bit quicker, not by much, and the eyeball moved slightly prior to the eye lids opening a bit more. I thought, 'I wonder if anyone has really looked at the process the eyes of the horse use?', 'Why, when I was moving slowly, did the horse not see me?', 'What in his eyes, or part of his brain, had shut down so that he did not see me?'. My brain works in that way, always asking questions.

The eyes operate completely independently of each other and operate independently of the ears. Many studies state that the ears point to where the attention of the horse's eyes are looking, however, my observations and the video footage I have acquired disprove this.

It is with the look of the eyes that we can see when a horse is not communicating to those around it, I go into detail with this in chapter twelve, with a glazed look and something in the brain appears to switch off.

One of the amazing things that was noted in my personal studies, which was caught on camera, is what the horse sees, especially when the sun is out and there are shadows on the ground.

I was standing with one of my horses, Pye, taking videos. I was so focused on the little screen I did not see a horse approaching Pye from behind, but I saw the ears change on Pye that alerted me that someone must be coming.

As I watched the video footage at home, the setting was as the horse approached, it was to the rear of Pye in his blind spot. He would not have physically seen the horse approaching him, however, you see Pye's iris look to the ground and there, reflected in Pye's eyeball, is a shadow of a horse. Pye was using the shadows on the ground to know what was coming from behind, truly fascinating to observe the horses use this aspect of thinking ability. In the shadow's silhouette you could see that the horse coming from behind had his ears in a forward position, which must have communicated to Pye the other horse's intention as he did not react to the approaching horse.

Now, bearing in mind Pye is the bossy one of the herd, normally if a horse comes up behind Pye and has intention, i.e. there is food about or something that Pye doesn't want, then Pye will react by first, communicating to the horse that is approaching him, and second, by moving his hind quarters towards the one approaching. In this scenario, Pye just stood completely still, he knew exactly what was going to happen with the horse behind because he had observed the positions of the ears of the horse coming from behind. It was in his blind spot, physically with his eyes he could not have seen it, however, by looking down to the ground and the shadows he could perfectly see the intentions of the horse by what was detailed in the shadows.

In what situations have you observed a horse respond to a situation that is outside of their field of view? What do you think the horse may have been responding to, to decide their actions or inactions?

Got questions about your horse, or the book?
Please submit at www.meljayturner.com

Chapter 12

—

Silence and the Neutral Face

*B*ooks and journals all look at aspects of glazed over faces or blank faces of the horse, all not fully signifying what it means as you read the information.

From my experience being with the herd, it just means *'Silence'* or *'I am quiet and not communicating with you'*. It is a look that is seen daily in the herd, whether they are resting, playing or in conversation, every now and then one or two of the horses' faces becomes a glazed stare and the facial muscles relax; they are not communicating to the other horses around them. They are still aware, but not communicating and their ear positions are always different depending on those near them.

It is the same when we see a horse standing still, waiting, and their faces seem blank, even though they might be looking directly towards us.

It is not often that you do not see horses communicating, especially when they are in a herd, there is always something happening, even when grazing. When they do stop communicating a completely different expression comes to their face as it relaxes.

When it comes to studies where pain is induced to horses to see what pain face they might pull, a glazed look comes over the eye, the eyes open wider and you can see muscular changes to the face as the muscles contract with the pain. I am sure we all can relate to hurting ourselves in accidents and having a glazed look in our eyes, it seems horses are no different in this area.

In what situations may you have observed a horse's neutral face? What was occurring in the environment around the horse at the time?

Got questions about your horse, or the book?
Please submit at www.meljayturner.com

Chapter 13

—

The Ears - Isolated Actions

One day, around the year 2015, I saw how much the ears were used to communicate as I was tending a client's herd and she had a new horse added to the field. As I entered the field, I knew there was an air about this horse that said she is higher in the ranking than the other horses. I went about seeing to the other horses and she stood watching. Then I turned to her and, in the way I had seen the horses do, I motioned I was coming to her.

First a look of surprise or even disbelief that I had just spoken to her in her language, then she responded she understood that I was coming to her. As I got closer, I requested to approach, a simple movement of the head that I had observed the horses do and that was it, a flood of ear actions I had never seen before. That was where the thought of the maritime semaphore flags came in play with the creating of the code. The isolated actions were so defined, I knew she had just taken my learning to a whole new level. I shook my head, which, as I have already said, also means '*No*' in the horse language. I lifted my hair and showed her my ears, pulling them around to show how useless they were in comparison. She leant forward, touched my ears, then started rubbing her ear all over my head. I had the camera in hand for that part, it was quite amazing. I learnt a lot from this horse, Quest was her name and that was applicable to what I have been doing. I was on a quest to understand what the horses say in detail.

Quest then started rubbing her ear all over my head.

Figure 11

Something, furthermore, started to catch my attention and that was the isolated actions of the ears. Not only from observation in the herd at the sanctuary, but also watching trainers such as Monty Roberts - the world-renowned horse whisperer who kindly provided a foreword to this book. I had seen it in his training program *Equus Online University* or within the round pen, to which I am an Ambassador of the Equus Online University. When a horse seemed confused its right ear would flick back and forth once, then stop. When the horse then seemed to understand what was required, the left ear would flick back and forth once, then stop, in the same way the right ear had done previously. Monty makes mention of this in one of his books, that he understands when the horse is going to do as it is asked and the left ear comes forward. I tested this out with the herd, asking them to do things that they had not done before, then as soon as they got it, the left ear signal would come.

Likewise, until they understood, which didn't take long, the right ear signal would come. So, I defined this to mean right ear '*I do not understand*' and left ear '*I understand*'. Once the horse gives the left ear signal, I know they are going to do what is asked. However, the more I watched both our herd and online video footage of trainers, with horses they'd never worked with before, it wasn't just an ears forward movement, but a series of two connected movements or of three set positions; a starting point forward; a middle point, backward; and an end point, forward again. No matter where the ears had been prior to this, it was always the same two connected movements or isolated actions, with a small-time gap before anything else happened. It is only when that left ear signal comes that the horses then proceed to do as the handler requests, mounting block scenarios are good examples.

Until then, the right ear will repeat the same pattern stating, '*I do not understand*', until they do understand. To me that would make sense as every action has an opposite action, we say, 'Hello' and we say, 'Goodbye'.

In my time at university I was watching the horses in the stables being put through various scenarios, especially in the therapy centre the right '*I do not understand*' ear action made it so obvious that these horses did not understand the new equipment they had to use, using the swimming pool for the first time or having to stand still in the water treadmill or spa.

One ear position that all horses need to be aware of, from very early in their life, is the 'alert' position. Using TESC it identifies it as 'TESC=(NS/OS(i)9(B)) frontal'. I say frontal as the ear has the capacity at number nine, on the lateral scale, to be facing forward, laterally or backward, they all have different meanings. Where the horses are situated at the time of writing this book, there are several areas where cars can pass, with wooded areas at both ends of the field and this ear action is seen quite often. What catches my attention, however, is not the horse that has gone to this 'TESC=(NS/OS(i)9(B)) frontal' alert ear action, but the herd around him or her. The horses around all keep grazing as the one to attention remains motionless in the 'alert' ear position, however, they all position their bodies to look towards the horse that is to attention. You can see the eyes looking towards the alert horse, all waiting for the next move. It is even better when you are looking through the lens of a zoom camera, it is not so visible with the naked eye unless you are there within the herd. When there is real concern, that horse will stay motionless and to attention until one of the other horses comes to attention also and looks for what could be causing concern, then between them you see a decision made if there is reason to flee or continue grazing. As much as we try to domesticate horses, we will never take that innate response to run when they need to.

I have lost count now of how much time I have spent in simply observing the herd and watching the videos back. Between 2011 and 2016, at the time of starting university, I'd calculated around 7,000 hours of observation of the horses. Adding the workload from university and the in-depth detail I had to watch and document for the dissertation, of the video footage of the horses, I lost track of how much time I had invested. In all, up to the time of writing this book I can easily say I have invested over 10,000 hours of learning in this area, of the horses' language, and my learning continues. Nevertheless, the more I watched, especially in slow motion, the more I could see the horses' language.

In what situations may you have observed a horse's right ear action of '*I do not understand*' and the left ear action of '*I understand*'? Have you observed any other repetitive actions of the horse's ears?

Got questions about your horse, or the book?
Please submit at www.meljayturner.com

Chapter 14

—

How Horses' Ears Enable Them to Avoid Colliding

When it came to direction, some of the actions were very clear. For one example, I was standing with my daughter's horse Seaton, face to face, generally chatting my thoughts and his right ear suddenly flicked out laterally, before turning his head to the right and walking away. I looked to my right and coming behind me was Pye, the bossy one of the field. Pye walking up behind me, to my right, bearing in mind Seaton was facing me, instigated Seaton's right ear turning to the right prior to walking away to his right.

Throughout all of my personal study and that of the dissertation, ear changes were connected with some form of action and movement. Even when group herding, you can see on the video footage the various ear position and changes alerting the horses around them depending on who was near them. The closer another horse, the closer the ear action position on the TESC coding to the (A) and (B) frontal positions and the direction in which they are going to take.

Bringing this to round penning a horse, the handlers will say that the horse's ears have now locked onto the handler. However, if they are using their ears to state direction, could it be that it is just saying I am now going in this direction? When you think about it, when a horse first goes into around pen it will look for a way out, but when it concedes that there is no escape, it will show what it will do next, be it left or the right. This being the case, if it were travelling to the left then the left ear would be in the direction towards the centre of the pen and vice versa if it was travelling to the right, the direction of its right ear would be in the direction towards to the centre of the pen. In effect the horse's ears are not locking onto the handler, the horse's ear is telling the direction in which it has chosen to travel or is having to travel.

The longer I watch the horses and watched the video footage back in slow motion, there more my attention was drawn to how the ears would change before the horse changed direction, from either a slight movement to an exaggerated movement. It was watching this that helped me see that the horses used their ears to show which direction they are going to take. I put this to the test very early on when the horses would charge around the field during group exercise time.

I was always taking photographs and videos when I trained and I would stand in the direct line of their path, as they came towards me each horse would alter their ear pattern. One ear in a forward direction, and the other ear in various points, but always backward. As they passed me their ear position would change again. Fascinating to watch as they came hurtling towards me. The more I focused on what the ears were doing, the more defined I saw the angles were that they used.

Chapter 15

—

The Ears and the
Stay Apparatus

Now I am going to throw a spanner into the works. Something I have found in studies and even chatting with a lady who actually dissects horses; a stay apparatus has never been identified. (For those who are not aware of horses, a stay apparatus is a method of the horses locking its ligaments and muscles to be able to stand still for long periods of time whilst dozing.) This stay apparatus is as also present in the horse's ears, which you can see when horses are fighting with each other, their ears can remain motionless at the same angle as the heads move.

This sparked my inquisitive mind. 'Do horses change their positions according to their head movements?'. The horses at the sanctuary are pretty used to Darrell and I having the camera around them and, after I get that look from the horses of '*Here she goes again*', I can view the horses through the lens without directly looking at them and they can carry on what they doing regardless of my gaze. As long as I look through the camera lens, they ignore me.

When they fight close to me, I choose to remain in a neutral state of mind. If people are visiting and the horses start to fight I intervene with a verbal '*Ha*', that catches their attention, and a warning look that makes them stop. When it is just Darrell and I, we allow them to continue fighting without interfering and it is during this time you can see that the ear movements remain at a similar angle irrelevant of how the head moves. This shows that there must be a stay apparatus in that the horse can manoeuvre its head where it chooses, while maintaining a position of its ears to communicate its intentions. It is fascinating to watch and we have lots of close up video footage of the horses fighting. From observation, the detail of the ear actions show there is communication there that has not yet been fully understood. You might think a fight is over, but the slightest ear action and it starts all over again.

You can practice this yourself with your arm and hand, hold your arm our straight with your hand flexed up like an ear, then raise your arm holding your hand in the same position. You will feel muscles working in your wrist but should be able to maintain the position of your hand as you raise your arm up and down. Basically, a locking system in order to maintain the hand or the horse's ear in the same position as it is moving its head around.

Chapter 16

—

Mimics and Mimes

*I*n these final few chapters I look at other aspects of horse communication that I think need elaborating on.

We know that horses comply with human requests and can learn multiple methods from multiple trainers. Trainers generally train through body language, which is what makes the horses so good at the jobs they are given to do. However, there are still areas that are not covered, especially when it comes to understanding what the horse is going to do next.

What was essential in learning the language of the horse over the years was to step back and watch, without imposing previous understanding of what I had been taught. It was during that time that I saw the mimics and mimes of our foal Raisin and noted how important this is to the training of domestic horse.

Horses can learn something just from observation and fast, with studies supporting observational learning within horses. Many successful trainers will use some form of mimicry in order to teach their horses. Horses love games and the more interesting you make it, the more likely you are to produce results.

If the horse is willing to work along with the trainer/ handler/rider, they will do almost do anything for them. The question is, though, how many current teachings support this? Or is force, used to gain control of the horse, still a mindset of many trainers?

Remember we take away the choice of a horse as soon as we trap it or put a head collar on it, so it is our responsibility to ensure that how we treat the horse from that point defines us as a person.

Horses learn no matter how they are taught, however, with absence of pain and violence a true partnership can be produced, which is reflected in not just how the horse performs, but also the expressions the horses produce while they are performing. If the horse looks like it is in pain because of its facial expression, with tight eyes and a frown to the brow, then the chances are you have it correct and the horse is really in pain.

Partnership involves both parties giving and taking, but rarely in horse training methods do you see the trainer doing something for the horse. It is nearly always the trainer giving the command and the horse having to comply. Will this ever change?

Chapter 17

—

Every Horse Has Its Place

*T*he horses we rescued, we offered permanent homes for horses. We were setting up as a charity, however, part of the rules in the UK is that horse charities have to re-home their horses and this would have stopped us offering permanent homes for horses that have been abused either mentally or physically. We ceased the idea of the charity and now fund the horses ourselves to provide a forever home for the horses, which is where this book, *The Equine Semaphore Code,* comes in for supporting them. All the horses have had to learn their social ranking. Some studies say there is none, because the herd does not follow every time a particular horse goes to food or water first, however my long-term observations shows that there is order within the ranks.

The youngest are always central to the herd

when 'at rest' if they want to move then the whole herd will adjust themselves to keep the young central. As the herd at the sanctuary grew, it was noted that the loudest is not always the hierarchy, it is the quietest both mare and geldings in our case. The louder, more dominant Pye demonstrated a role of protecting the hierarchy mare and gelding/stallion at the sanctuary. This has also been shown in studies, but not from the perspective that the bossy stallion is protecting the hierarchy, but allowing the other stallions to be within the herd, yet there remains a lack of understanding why a bossy stallion allows a quieter one to remain there. Many of these observations are short studies and without a baseline for reference.

Observing the herd, as it grew, the quietest lead, not to water or food, but by maintaining order within the herd. They exhibit a leadership that only requires a look or a flick of the tail for the intention to be understood and carried out, all very clear the longer you observe, even to the point that you can see the hierarchy mare or stallion/gelding give an intention look or command, through the flick of the ear or movement of the body, to the bossy one and the bossy one will start to herd the horses in the direction they have been told to do. At the time of writing this book, my obsession you could say, was observing, for seven years, watching, learning, and implementing. Mares all have the capacity to lead and it is amazing to see the mares sort their ranking as they will have a face-off and urinate at the same time while looking at each other, their facial expressions are quite expressive also. Of the mares that we have had come into the herd, I wish I had this on video footage, it is quite fascinating to watch as they challenge each other with these facial expressions and urination processes.

When a new horse comes into the field, or a horse passes away, this changes the hierarchy of the herd and the whole herd needs to re-establish the hierarchy again.

When it comes to males that are the loudest seeming to be the hierarchy, it is not until you observe and look closer at this that the loud ones are actually protecting the hierarchy pair, who tend to be the quiet members of the herd. This becomes clear when the mares come into season and then the hierarchy has his say.

For us at the sanctuary it is Barney, the Shetland, who is the quiet hierarchy, but when it comes to the mares being in season, he will fight dirty to win. With precision he first takes out his opponent's knee, which makes them drop to the ground, then rearing, he aims at biting the eye. Fights with Barney are fast and are over in seconds before the herd moves away. He is rarely challenged at those times of year; however, newer horses have to learn the hard way.

We rarely see the protector Pye and the hierarchy Barney fight, however, when they do it is vicious and Pye always loses from acquired injuries. So there is a hierarchy system, but not what I've read in journals or books that have been based on short term studies, with human opinions. What I have come to view over a long time, seeing what hierarchy is but in the manner of true leadership those taking the lead speak when needed and others are ready to follow.

Figure 12a

Barney knows how to win fights.

Figure 12b

Figure 12c

Dakota is the predominate lead mare in the herd and I have only seen her speak out twice in five years at the time of writing this. When she does speak, even the protector gets out of her way, it is fascinating to watch as she is tiny in comparison.

Chapter 18

—

Our Ears Are Not
Like A Horse's!

A particular horse's silent neutral face has saved me in several circumstances, especially when dealing with horses that have become aggressive to their owners. What I often do is, I also assume a silent, neutral face and this allows the horse to see that I have no aggressive intent towards them. To these horses, being quiet in body, face and mind is essential for helping them to understand the human request. The same when handling feral horses, that quietness at first is essential for gaining trust quickly and calmly.

Horses recognise varieties of training without the need for action from human ears. Horse training techniques vary all around the world and the horse manages to learn all of them and have an effective working relationship with humans. That is some skill, denoting high intelligence and memory capabilities.

Using of our facial expressions, the movement of our body, legs, and head we can communicate like a horse. We can emulate all of the eye, tongue, body and leg movements of *The Equine Semaphore Code*. It is the learning of how the horse puts this code into action that allows us to formulate the science behind the equine language.

With our lack of ear manoeuvrability, which my studies have shown provide a communication system plus it is used to show the direction the horse is going to take, we can use our arms for direction or hands for a more subtle signal, like how the horse uses its ears. Many horse trainers already do this and, without thinking about it, everyone who handles a horse already does, however, it is the horse that picks up on how the arms and hands are used.

Horses quickly pick up different training methods. Working a horse with the use of my arms, imitating the horse's ears and how they use it for communicating direction, the horse can pick up on the first meeting that our arms are able to indicate direction. I noticed this at university in the way we were taught to hold the reins while leading a horse. Standing beside the horse's head you instinctively raise your arm when you prepare to move the horse on, the horse recognises this as a directional signal to walk forwards and it does. If you walk in front of the horse your arm goes backwards, similar to a horse's ear when it is stationary, and your horse refuses to come forward. From my observations, the horse understands a backwards arm to mean '*Do not come forward*'. I wish I could show you the video footage of it happening, but the videos I have of that were for use at university and not for the public.

Add arm and hand positioning, to facial expressions and body language, and a conversation has started before you have reached the horse's side, even if you are unaware of it.

We lack the use of the pinna-shaped ears; however, horses can otherwise learn almost anything from their trainers. They soon started to understand that I was trying to use my arms and hands to duplicate what the horses were doing with their ears, to a degree. As I watch other people with horses, I noted that horses had already connected the movement of human arms as a form of signal and were responding to what they were interpreting from the actions. I know I am only touching the surface with this book, but here it is - a language between the horses that we as humans can learn and utilise. Take into account that we consider ourselves the most intelligent beings on the planet, because of what we have physically achieved. We can take the time to learn multiple human languages in detail. We teach French, Spanish, German and more in our high schools. Now you could learn a newly documented language that allows us to communicate with a non-human species!

Chapter 19

—

Horses Are Sentient Beings

*H*orses, like many animals, are clearly sentient beings in the dictionary sense of being responsive to, or conscious of, sense impressions. Just because some foolish humans think that only people have feelings and true sentient thought, should not blind us to the truth: humans are only one of the sentient species on this planet.

In fact, horses are particularly sensitive and intelligent creatures, capable of all the following feelings and more.

- Concern
- Love
- Affection
- Anger

- Jealousy
- Awkwardness
- Embarrassment
- Reactive
- Understanding
- Cheeky
- Playfulness

All these characteristics I have seen in horses that I have helped.

All animals have a communication system, but, apart from the odd few, the human animal still fails to learn the non-human animal communication. Horses can communicate with facial expressions and body language, but when you connect the variations of the ear actions with the facial expression and the variations and repetitions in the vocal expressions, a whole new picture comes into view.

Horses can learn different human languages and with the way horses are bred in one country then moved to another for sales, the horse learns quickly the new changes to the words such as 'Woah', 'Trot', 'Stand', etc. New owners are always taking for granted that the horse might have been taught

Dutch with its breeders, but then here we expect it to understand the words in our language immediately.

Horses can comprehend human words and follow out requested actions, understand the names we give them and every training method possible to the desire of its trainer. We do not credit the horse with the level of intelligence it really has.

One aim of this book is to start raising questions as to the rights of animals that can show human emotions and what they can communicate to us. Do the differences of what we look like, or our species, mean that we should not all be treated equally? If an alien species landed, would we treat them like we do our animals, just because they might look different to us? We would still have to learn the alien language.

The whole world operates in harmony with each other, except the human species. Only the human species destroys for material gain, whereas the non-human species work in accord to their daily needs. This needs to change if our future is to survive.

Animals have a language system that can be learnt and understood by humans, but it is the blindness of humans that keep the animals in a more vulnerable position. Their willingness to comply with humans puts them in a vulnerable position, when it comes to the meat chain, and they have no idea what awaits them. They just know they are getting fed and living in the now each day. A question I always ask myself, why did we start eating our fellow beings, were we copying other animals?

Chapter 20

—

What Next?

*A*s for me, I will keep learning the language of the horse. For the scientific minded who might be reading this, further research needs to be done. I hope as a reader that my book will encourage you to search even more.

From a human and equine perspective, we need to be working more efficiently and always be looking for improvements for our non-human counterparts.

By living as part of a herd for many years, I have come to learn to communicate with the horses using their language. This includes the sounds they use, tongue movements, as much as my tongue will allow, and implementing my hand movements to replicate ear movements. Video footage would be required of horses behaving in a natural environment, to create an ethogram of all the actions, not just commonly understood ones.

The ethogram, created in my dissertation for this book, of the ears is just a fraction of what is needed to create a bigger ethogram putting all the signals together. Horses are not moving their ears around for no reason and it is not only connected with listening.

The eyes are a massive part of the horse's communication system, when connected with the other aspects of the ears, the mouth and the tongue, the eyes become an expression to support the other actions.

The ears, as described in this book are a big source of the communication system, not only telling the other horses the direction they are moving in, but also telling the other horses where they want them to go. It is all in the facial expression whether they are saying, '*I am going that way*' or saying, '*You go that way*'.

Until a full code is recorded, the language of the horse will still be overlooked. The human animal will continue to think they are clever, teaching their horses to understand symbols and respond to human words or be submitted to painful scenarios to see what expression they might pull. While this is happening, the horse will keep waiting patiently for us to catch up.

Just because they are not designed to write and read and develop technology, does not mean they lack intelligence. For the intelligence of the horse, it usually takes three or four repetitions before they have learnt it. Some horses go through many owners and learn the behaviour and requests of each owner. Skilled horse riders know that being precise with every action is key to the horse's performance, but also know that as soon as they get a horse that they have not ridden before, the first part of the ride involves teaching the horse how they ride, so the horse can adjust to the slight differences of the human riding.

Living with horses as much as possible was my goal and has taught me more than I could have learnt in books or scientific articles. As I move forward with my research, the herd at the sanctuary have already accepted me as one of them, despite the physical differences, and I move in and around with them as part of the herd and all the benefits that go with being part of a herd.

Do not get me wrong, I still realise the weaknesses of being human around horses, however, with learning the language of the horse, which is ongoing, I have been able to become part of the herd. The respect they have for each other and the boundaries they have in place, can be duplicated from a human point of view while in the herd, but is also an amazing example of what we can learn between ourselves as a human race. Remembering always that the hierarchy within the herd is not the loudest, but the quietest, only becoming loud when important things need to be determined. That alone should be another study.

Further work...

A complete documented system would be required, that takes into account all of the actions a horse expresses, to fully understand what the horses are communicating between themselves. The dissertation for my BSc, looked at identifying the 'at rest' ear position and reason for the variations of it. Oh, I forgot to say earlier, the results of my dissertation had a highly significant conclusion ($p<0.00001$) that horses do not have an 'at rest' ear position. Of the twelve ear positions identified during the video footage at rest, every ear action was preceded with another action of the horse, signifying communication or language.

In my study, it identified that the horse's ear

positions are strategically placed at angles as part of their communication, something that is scientifically measurable when set markers are applied, hence *The Equine Semaphore Code.*

Understanding how they communicate with each other will give a deeper insight into the horse/human relationship and an opportunity to improve the rider's performance, by understanding what the horse is going to do next. The dissertation study focused on two-dimensional footage, which gives limited range for a detailed study of all the actions the horse's ears perform.

Further studies would need to focus on three-dimensional footage or use digital technology to obtain a more accurate analysis of the ranges of the individual ear actions the horses use. With the progression in technology, we now possess the ability to join together all of the actions that studies have found, expanding to include head actions, ears movements, eyes and tongue movement in everyday scenarios, to help create a bigger picture.

Further studies, in developing TESC and other facial coding systems in order that people can learn to understand what the horses is saying.

My dissertation study focused on only one aspect of the horse's ear position, which detailed that it is not just an 'at rest' ear position or action but had greater meaning within the equine communication system. Yet there are many more actions and patterns to the horse's ear movements that require observation.

In the results it was noted that the horse seemed to indicate a direction prior to taking that action with its ears, if it was turning to the left its ear would turn left first, with the head and body following, and vice versa to the right.

In a ridden scenario, this would prove valuable as a rider approaches a jump to know if the horse is deciding to run out or go over the jump.

Currently high-speed cameras are being used for data collection of muscle movements, in aid of understanding the biomechanics of horses. It would be beneficial for digital high-speed imaginary collected to collate detailed ear movement and their connection between the actions of the horse.

Adding a handler into the studies after a completed code is achieved, we will be able to ascertain how the horse if fully responding or communicating to its handler on the ground. With taking it further to ridden studies, how the horse responds to ridden requests and considering this study has identified the horse's ears move into a backward position just before stopping, how this relates to the actions of horses that stop during riding or refuse to go over jumps.

Looking at Rolkur, a riding method that pulls the horses chin close to the horses chest, giving the neck of the horse a curled action which some consider a beautiful action, however, studies have proven that this method of forcing the horses head and holding it in this position is damaging to the cervical spine of the horse – it is another area that TESC would identify if it meets the needs and five freedoms of the horse. My calculations say it does and that horses are being prevented from communicating its intentions. When applying TESC, you can see not only a very angry horse ear position, but also that the horse's ear is twisted in a way that is totally unnatural, always with a human sitting on top having the capability of smiling while causing suffering.

I think we owe it to these amazing animals to learn more about them and see how they want to work with us. They are happy to work with us, that is clear to see, but imagine what could be achieved if that barrier of miscommunication was broken.

Figure 13

THE END

Got questions about your horse, or the book?
Please submit at www.meljayturner.com

Your Thoughts and Experience

WARNING!
Protected by Copyright Law
All Rights Reserved

You are not allowed to
make copies of this work
without the owner's permission

Registered & Certified by
Protectmywork.com

REFERENCES
Research connected with
The Equine Semaphore Code.

Balter, M. (2010) 'Animal Communication Helps Reveal Roots of Language'. Science, 328(5981), pp.969-971.

Benhajali, H., Richard-Yris, M., Leroux, M., Ezzaouia, M., Charfi, F. and Hausberger, M. (2008) 'A note on the time budget and social behaviour of densely housed horses: A case study in Arab breeding mares'. Applied Animal Behaviour Science, 112(1-2), pp.196-200. https://doi.org/10.1016/j.applanim.2007.08.007.

Bethell, Henry Arthur. (1861) Modern Guns and Gunnery, 1910: A Practical Manual for Officers of the Horse, Field and Mountain Artillery. Woolwich, Cattermole. p.255 (Bethell, 1861).

British Sign Language (2019). Learn British Sign Language. [online] British Sign Language - Learn BSL Online. Available at: https:// www.british-sign.co.uk/ [Accessed 24 Apr. 2018].

Brubaker, L. and Udell, M. (2016) 'Cognition and learning in horses (Equus caballus): What we know and why we should ask more'. Behavioural Processes, 126, pp.121-131.

Caeiro, C., Waller, B., Zimmermann, E., Burrows, A. and DavilaRoss, M. (2012) 'OrangFACS: A Muscle-Based Facial Movement Coding System for Orangutans (Pongo spp.). 'International Journal of Primatology, 34(1), pp.115-129.

Caeiro, C., Burrows, A., and Waller, B. (2017) 'Development and application of CatFACS: Are human cat adopters influenced by cat facial expressions?,' Applied Animal Behaviour Science, 189, pp.66-78.

Dalla Costa, E., Minero, M., Lebelt, D., Stucke, D., Canali, E. and Leach, M. (2014) 'Development of the Horse Grimace Scale (HGS) as a Pain Assessment Tool in Horses Undergoing Routine Castration'. PLoS ONE, 9(3), p.e92281.

Dyson, S. (2015) 'Evaluation of poor performance in competition horses: A musculoskeletal perspective. Part 1: Clinical assessment'. Equine Veterinary Education, 28(5), pp.284-293.

Dyson, S. and Van Dijk, J. (2018) 'Application of a ridden horse ethogram to video recordings of 21 horses before and after diagnostic analgesia: Reduction in behaviour scores'. Equine Veterinary Education.

Dyson, S., Berger, J., Ellis, A. and Mullard, J. (2018) 'Behavioral observations and comparisons of nonlame horses and lame horses before and after resolution of lameness by diagnostic analgesia'. Journal of Veterinary Behavior, 26, pp.64-70.

Dyson, S., Berger, J., Ellis, A. and Mullard, J. (2018) 'Development of an ethogram for a pain scoring system in ridden horses and its application to determine the presence of musculoskeletal pain'. Journal of Veterinary Behavior, 23, pp.47-57.

Dyson, S. (2016) 'Evaluation of poor performance in competition horses: A musculoskeletal perspective. Part 2: Further investigation. Equine Veterinary Education, 28(7), pp.379-387'.

Ekman P, Friesen WV, Hager JC (2002) The facial action coding system. Salt Lake City: Research Nexus.

Elgersma, A., Wijnberg, I., Sleutjens, J., Van Der Kolk, J., Van Weeren, P. and Back, W. (2010) 'A pilot study on objective quantification and anatomical modelling of in vivo head and neck positions commonly applied in training and competition of sport horses'. Equine Veterinary Journal, 42, pp.436-443.

Frith, C. (2009). 'Role of facial expressions in social interactions'. Philosophical Transactions of the Royal

Society B: Biological Sciences, 364(1535), pp.3453-3458.

Fritz, C. (2012). A Journey through the Horse's Body. Richmond: Cadmos Publishing Limited, p.27.

Gleerup, K. and Lindegaard, C. (2015)' Recognition and quantification of pain in horses: A tutorial review,' Equine Veterinary Education, 28(1), pp.47-57. https://doi.org/10.1111/eve.12383.

Goodwin, D., McGreevy, P., Waran, N., McLean, A., 2009 'How equitation science canelucidate and refine horsemanship techniques'. Vet. J. 181, 5e11.

Górecka-Bruzda, A., Kosińska, I., Jaworski, Z., Jezierski, T. and Murphy, J. (2015) 'Conflict behavior in elite show jumping and dressage horses'. Journal of Veterinary Behavior, 10(2), pp.137-146.

Hall, C. and Heleski, C. (2017) 'The role of the ethogram in equitation science'. Applied Animal Behaviour Science, 190, pp.102-110.

Hall, C., Kay, R. and Yarnell, K. (2014) 'Assessing ridden horse behavior: Professional judgment and physiological measures'. Journal of Veterinary Behavior, 9(1), pp.22-29.

Jankunis, E. and Whishaw, I. (2013). Sucrose Bobs and Quinine Gapes: Horse (Equus caballus) responses to taste support phylogenetic similarity in taste reactivity. Behavioural Brain Research, 256, pp.284-290.

Kainer, R. (1993) 'Clinical Anatomy of the Equine Head'. Veterinary Clinics of North America: Equine Practice, 9(1), pp.1-23.

Kimura, R. (1997) 'Mutual grooming and preferred associate relationships in a band of free-ranging horses'. Applied Animal Behaviour Science, 59, pp.265-276.

Lambert, H. and Carder, G. (2018) 'Positive and negative emotions in dairy cows: Can ear postures be used as a measure?'. Behavioural Processes, 158, pp.172-180.

Lesimple, C., Fureix, C., De Margerie, E., Sénèque, E., Menguy, H. and Hausberger, M. (2012). Towards a Postural Indicator of Back Pain in Horses (Equus caballus). PLoS ONE, 7(9), p.e44604.

Ludewig, A., Gauly, M. and König von Borstel, U. (2013) 'Effect of shortened reins on rein tension, stress and discomfort behavior in dressage horses'. Journal of Veterinary Behavior, 8(2), pp.e15-e16.

McIlwraith, C. and Rollin, B. (2011) Equine welfare. Chichester, UK: Wiley-Blackwell.

Mullard, J., Berger, J., Ellis, A. and Dyson, S. (2017) 'Development of an ethogram to describe facial expressions in ridden horses (FEReq)'. Journal of Veterinary Behavior, 18, pp.7-12. (Nestadt et al., 2015).

Parr, L., Waller, B., Vick, S. and Bard, K. (2007). Classifying chimpanzee facial expressions using muscle action. Emotion, 7(1), pp.172-181.

Pearce, John.M. (ed.) (2008) Animal Learning & Cognition: An Introduction. Hove. Psychology Press.

Proctor, H. and Carder, G. (2014) 'Can ear postures reliably measure the positive emotional state of cows?'. Applied Animal Behaviour Science, 161, pp.20-27.

Proops, L. and McComb, K. (2012) 'Cross-modal individual recognition in domestic horses (Equus caballus) extends to familiar humans'. Proceedings of the Royal Society B: Biological Sciences, 279 (1741), pp.3131-3138.

Randle, H. (2016) 'Welfare friendly equitation - Understanding horses to improve training and performance'. Journal of Veterinary Behavior, 15, p.vii-viii.

Randle, H., Steenbergen, M., Roberts, K. and Hemmings, A. (2017) 'The use of the technology in equitation science: A panacea or abductive science?'. Applied Animal Behaviour Science, 190, pp.57-73.

Ransom, J. and Cade, B.S (2009) Quantifying equid behavior— A research ethogram for free-roaming feral horses: U.S. Geological Survey Techniques and Methods 2-A9, p.23.

Marcet Rius, M., Pageat, P., Bienboire-Frosini, C., Teruel, E., Monneret, P., Leclercq, J., Lafont-Lecuelle, C. and Cozzi, A. (2018). Tail and ear movements as possible indicators of emotions in pigs. Applied Animal Behaviour Science, 205, pp.14-18.

Schmelzer, A. (2003). Horse talk: The Langauge of Horses. Brunsbek, Germany: Cadmos. Sisson, S., Grossman, J. and Getty, R. (1975). The anatomy of the domestic animals. Philadelphia: W.B. Saunders. P379-386.

Smiet, E., Van Dierendonck, M., Sleutjens, J., Menheere, P., van Breda, E., de Boer, D., Back, W., Wijnberg, I. and van der Kolk, J. (2014) 'Effect of different head and neck positions on behaviour, heart rate variability and cortisol levels in lunged Royal Dutch Sport horses'. The Veterinary Journal, 202(1), pp.26-32.

Smith, A., Proops, L., Grounds, K., Wathan, J. and McComb, K. (2016) 'Functionally relevant responses to human facial expressions of emotion in the domestic horse (Equus caballus)'. Biology Letters, 12(2), p.20150907.

Smith, A., Proops, L., Grounds, K., Wathan, J., Scott, S. and McComb, K. (2018) 'Domestic horses (Equus caballus) discriminate between negative and positive human nonverbal vocalisations'. Scientific Reports, 8(1).

Waller, B., Peirce, K., Caeiro, C., Scheider, L., Burrows, A., McCune, S. and Kaminski, J. (2013) 'Paedomorphic Facial Expressions Give Dogs a Selective Advantage'. PLoS ONE, 8(12), p.e82686.

Warren-Smith, A., Greetham, L. and McGreevy, P. (2007). Behavioral and physiological responses of horses (Equus caballus) to head lowering. Journal of Veterinary Behavior, 2(3), pp.59-67.

Wathan, J. and McComb, K. (2014). The eyes and ears are visual indicators of attention in domestic horses. Current Biology, 24(15), pp.R677-R679.

Wathan, J., Burrows, Anne.M., Waller, Bridget.M., and McComb, Karen. (2015). EquiFACS: 'The Equine

Facial Action Coding System'. PLoS ONE 10(9): e0137818.

Weeren, P. and Crevier-Denoix, N. (2006) Equine conformation: clues to performance and soundness?. Equine Veterinary Journal, 38(7), pp.591-596.

Wilsie, S. (2018) 'Horses in Translation: Essential Lessons in Horse Speak: Learn to Listen and Talk in Their Language'. Vermont: Trafalgar Square. pp.31,32,39

Yule, G (ed.) (2014) The Study of Language. Cambridge: Cambridge University Press.